THE CASE FOR EUROPE

THE CASE FOR EUROPE

Unity, Diversity, and Democracy in the European Union

Philippe de Schoutheete

translated by Andrew Butler

LYNNE
RIENNER
PUBLISHERS

BOULDER
LONDON

Published in the United States of America in 2000 by
Lynne Rienner Publishers, Inc.
1800 30th Street, Boulder, Colorado 80301
www.rienner.com

and in the United Kingdom by
Lynne Rienner Publishers, Inc.
3 Henrietta Street, Covent Garden, London WC2E 8LU

First published in French as *Une Europe pour Tous* © 1997 by Editions Odile Jacob.
English-language translation © 2000 by Lynne Rienner Publishers, Inc.

Library of Congress Cataloging-in-Publication Data
Schoutheete, Philippe de, 1932–
   [Europe pour tous. English]
   The case for Europe : unity, diversity, and democracy in the European
Union / Philippe de Schoutheete.
     p. cm.
   Includes bibliographical references and index.
   ISBN 1-55587-898-9 (hc)
   ISBN 1-55587-900-4 (pb)
   1. European Union.   I. Title.
JN30 .S3713   2000
341.242'2—dc21   99-089753

British Cataloguing in Publication Data
A Cataloguing in Publication record for this book
is available from the British Library.

Printed and bound in the United States of America

 The paper used in this publication meets the requirements
of the American National Standard for Permanence of
Paper for Printed Library Materials Z39.48-1984.

5 4 3 2 1

CONTENTS

Foreword, Jacques Delors   ix

Foreword, Stanley Hoffmann   xv

Introduction   1

1   Concept and Action   3
    The Community and the Council of Europe
    The Community and Politics
    The Importance of Efficiency
    Majority Voting

2   Empire and Nation   13
    A Community Without Obligation
    A Community Without Hegemony
    A Specific Institutional Structure
    The Community and Nationalism

3   Structure and Network   23
    The Originality of the Structure
    The Legislature and the Executive
    Various Forms of Europe
    The Network

CONTENTS

4　Law and Politics　　　　　　　　　　　　　　　33
　　The Importance of Law
　　Direct Effect and Supremacy
　　The Luxembourg Compromise
　　Implicit Agreements

5　Subsidiarity and Intervention　　　　　　　　41
　　The Origin of the Concept
　　Subsidiarity and Maastricht
　　Noninterference and Intervention
　　Headlights, Cheese, and Beaches
　　Difficulties of Application

6　Democracy and Communication　　　　　　　51
　　The Democracy Deficit
　　The European Parliament and National Parliaments
　　Legality and Legitimacy
　　Transparency
　　Various Forms of Opacity

7　Cohesion and Diversity　　　　　　　　　　　61
　　Cohesion
　　Diversity
　　The Example of Monetary Union
　　The Challenge of Enlargement
　　Diversity and Differentiation

8　Power and Impotence　　　　　　　　　　　　71
　　Original Impotence
　　Political Cooperation
　　The Community and the Cold War
　　Currency
　　External Policy
　　Security and Defense

9　Competition and Solidarity　　　　　　　　　85
　　Cycles of Consensus
　　The Postwar Consensus

CONTENTS

The Durability and Effectiveness of the Postwar Consensus
The Neoliberal Consensus
Where Is the Compromise to Be Found?

10   The End and the Means   97
        A Lack of Debate on Objectives
        Confusion Between the End and the Means
        The History of European Construction
        Differentiation and Enlargement
        The Soul

Bibliography   109
Index   115
About the Book   118

FOREWORD

Jacques Delors

The labyrinths of the European Union are full of promises and disappointments. To enter, an informed guide is required. Ambassador Philippe de Schoutheete is that guide, equipped with vast knowledge and unequaled professional experience that he has acquired through active and long-standing involvement in European affairs.

His profound and unfailing faith in the ideal of a united Europe by no means detracts from his lucidity in helping us to penetrate the welter of information and to distinguish real from virtual, truth from falsehood, and promises made from what may be harsh reality.

The original edition of this book was published a few weeks after the European Council meeting in Amsterdam (17 June 1997), which witnessed the adoption of a new treaty and the confirmation of the previous commitments to achieve economic and monetary union.

As a basic clarification, it is worth recalling that the Treaty of Amsterdam merely amends and extends the existing treaties. A future codification of these treaties is essential, but in its absence, it is virtually impossible for the average citizen to understand the imbroglio of legislative texts. All the more reason to follow the guide, who provides us with material for thought by turning the spotlight on some essential topics, presented in pairs, linked either by dialectic or by opposition.

The path he follows implies frequent flashbacks to the history of Europe. Without that it would be impossible to understand either Europe's originality in relation to other countries or regional groupings, or the demons that torment it, or indeed the historical references that are so frequently used to bolster opposition to European integration. The origins of certain reactions will, however, emerge more clearly when considering the historical significance of the concepts of empire and nation. That is the starting point of the idea that the European venture is justified by the will to avoid all hegemony, whether exercised by an external power or by one or other of the member states.

If that demonstration fails to dispel the skepticism of the modern apostles of nationalism, I would invite them to consider the discussion on the relationship between law and politics. As emphasized by the author, "Law and politics mingle and are mutually supportive."

It is true that the European Union, or at least its Community pillar, is founded on two clear principles: direct effect of European law and its precedence over national law. It is not just a matter of efficiency, easily justified by the creation and proper working of a common economic area. European law should also be considered as a means of enabling sovereign states to live together and to act jointly, without needing prior intergovernmental discussions.

These principles of law constitute the nation-state's guarantee that the joint exercise of sovereignty will indeed be confined to the spheres that are clearly defined in the treaty. They also provide protection for the citizen, who can resort to the Court of Justice to confirm or re-establish his or her rights. The Treaty of Amsterdam—and this is one of its few positive aspects—has recently extended those rights, thus contributing to the gradual creation of a European public space.

Returning to that obsessive concept of Europe as a "destroyer" of nations and, in contrast, to the guarantees offered by a European legal system, Philippe de Schoutheete invites us to ponder the distinction between subsidiarity and intervention. Thus, he sheds light on the debate that Europeans have been wrestling with for several years concerning the optimal distribution of powers between the European level on the one hand and the national and regional levels on the other. Subsidiarity is a fine concept, as old as the Reformation that put it forward before the Catholic Church in turn sought to make use of it. The debate on this subject is full of hypocrisy and lies, as you will see—hence the current embarrassment of the member states, which, by invoking subsidiarity, often sought to veil their attachment to corporatist interests or to rekindle the fears of their citizens. This, incidentally, finally dismisses a number of artificial nightmares, as is clearly illustrated by the French commotion over raw milk cheeses.

Yet nothing is clearly settled, and it is understandable that the "man in the street" wants to know who does what and who is answerable to the electorate. From that point of view, I have always emphasized both the merits of a federal approach to the institutional problem and the vital necessity of reinforcing national cohesion, which has been weakened by the erosion of basic solidarities and by the absence of a visible and recognized enemy. Thank you, Europe, at least for that legacy of peace among us!

The political object taking shape before our eyes has no precedent in the history of institutions. It is all the more complex on that account because it is difficult to forget Montesquieu and to theorize on the networklike heterogeneous entity that has emerged particularly from the Maastricht and Amsterdam Treaties. As the author admits, it is "difficult to describe and to explain. It has no emotive value." That is the substance of the most vital issue to be considered.

How can one relate to this complex and technical Europe? How can one get involved in it? In the name of what objectives? Power— but its necessity and feasibility must first be explained. Competition—which implies unity and brings strength. Solidarity— which is already evident to a greater extent than is believed in common policies.

This brings us back to a classic dilemma of politics in a democracy. Building a united Europe requires historical analysis and a long-term vision. Who, in this "fast food" world, still has the will, the courage, and the ability to lead a nation toward that horizon, despite the difficulties of the moment and the various sacrifices that, in any case, will need to be made in the interests of survival?

The task is huge and work has barely begun. We need to explain Europe, its ends and its means, through the education we offer to the young, and we need to invent simplicity so as to render the stakes more comprehensible and the operation of the system more accessible to the average citizen. To achieve that, we must first abandon the easy option of finding a scapegoat: in this case, the nebula of "Brussels," concealing institutions and responsibilities, an alibi to sweeten any bitter pill.

It is not surprising, under the circumstances, that the credibility of the European venture decreases with each downturn of the economy and, more seriously today, in the face of our inability to fight against mass unemployment and a return to poverty.

I am firmly convinced that the problem is also rooted in the poor functioning of our national democracies; in nationalism, which invites each of us to retreat into our own niche; in audiovisual voyeurism, which will sometimes bring you to tears but later will reinforce your skepticism.

Nevertheless, because some of us are convinced that the union of European countries constitutes the condition of our survival, let us not retreat into the elitist stance of "those who were right, but who were misunderstood"; let us continue the fight, and above all, let us shed light on it strongly and in all clarity.

Why was the political part of the Maastricht Treaty ill conceived and ultimately inoperative? Why does the Treaty of Amsterdam in fact conceal a fiasco: the inability to conceive and define the framework of a European Union that has a historic duty to extend to our brothers and sisters in Eastern and Central Europe, too long separated from us by a disastrous decree of history? Because we can no longer distinguish the ends from the means! The single market with no internal borders and the single currency are in fact just means. What matters is, why are we fighting for this? Or, if you prefer, what are the objectives of our common enterprise? Had that question been raised in plain terms at the beginning of the latest intergovernmental conference, the masks would ultimately have dropped. A crisis would have arisen. It would have been of greater value than this mediocre and partial compromise.

On reading this book, you will discover the answer, or rather the answers, to that vital question. I hope that our political leaders may draw inspiration from it and, with a surge of lucidity and courage, confront the real issues. In the meantime, let us help them by informing public opinion. Let us help them by suggesting appropriate solutions. We will thereby contribute to the construction of a Europe that is united but rich in its diversity; strong because of its solidarity; powerful and generous and therefore influential.

FOREWORD

Stanley Hoffmann

Philippe de Schoutheete's book is only one among dozens of volumes devoted to the study of the European Union. But it has one overwhelming merit that distinguishes it from so many others: it goes to the heart of the decisive issues, it focuses on essentials. On the often Byzantine uniqueness of the Union's institutional structure, on the complex relationship between those institutions and the national publics, on the challenge of diversity in this quasi-federation of nation states (as Delors has called it), on the difficult leap from issues of welfare, trade, and money to issues of foreign policy and defense, de Schoutheete displays a remarkable talent for combining a penetrating and shrewd analysis with a firm sense of the new Europe's unfinished mission.

I would like to draw attention to his conclusions. They point to the tension between the method that has made possible the gradual development of the Union, in geographical and in functional scope—a focus on small steps, pragmatic compromises, and the setting up of specific policies and complicated procedures—and the ultimate purpose of the whole enterprise. The method can be defended easily: the participants never would have been able to agree on a common vision or design; progress could only come stealthily, with each member believing that its chances for determining the ultimate shape of the Union were intact. But the costs have been high. At every stage, the clash of visions manifests itself, so to speak, behind the stage. Also, as the scope of the enterprise expands, it becomes increasingly difficult to keep it away from the anxieties and doubts of the people whose fate it now so deeply affects, and to continue to treat it as the preserve of a small group of elites (political figures, bureaucrats, pressure group leaders—the producers rather than the consumers).

The institutional system, with its mix of democratic and technocratic agencies, has the virtue (if this is the right word) of being capable of either being pushed in a more federal direction or remaining as remote from the public and dominated by governments and their deals as the "sovereignists" of various countries still wish it to be. The limited results of the Amsterdam Treaty's attempt at reform—the essentially intergovernmental nature of the incipient foreign and defense policy—show how hard it remains to move in a more federal direction. Those who, like Jacques Delors and Philippe de Schoutheete, wish the Union to go in this direction have to take some formidable difficulties into account. One of these is the likely effects of enlargement. It is now clear that in a few years we will have a Union of twenty or twenty-one members, with six or seven more knocking at the door. To be sure, the present institutions can be reformed so that an increase in the number of members does not provoke a breakdown; but no reform can conceal the fact that the more members there are, the less likely it is that unity of vision and an agreement on final design can be obtained. There may well have to be a differentiation between a "hard core" and laggards, as de Schoutheete recognizes.

A second problem is that there can be no real federal Europe, no truly meaningful European citizenship, unless the Parliament becomes truly European in its mode of selection and campaigning. There can be no European nation, but there could be a federation of nations—if the common institutions are not simply a juxtaposition of national ministers helped by a common bureaucracy and flanked by an assembly chosen after an election waged almost exclusively on national issues. Thus, what is needed is the creation of a European public space, with common debates on common issues. So far, public space has remained national. How willing are governments to create a common, European, public space? How willing are the media to "Europeanize" their coverage, the parties to form, at the European level, more than marriages of convenience? The multiplicity of languages does not help.

Third, for the European Union to become a "complete" power in the world, after so many years as a "civilian" power, much more will be needed than a high official in charge of common defense and diplomatic policies and a more frequent resort to qualified majority voting in the Council. Kosovo may have had an effect on the EU comparable to that of the Suez crisis on the Community in the late 1950s, but three formidable obstacles remain: The smaller members show far less eagerness than the bigger ones in this domain; the costs of an effective military program are high, and the states that would have to pay most are handicapped by the famous requirements of monetary stability set up for the creation of EMU, as well as by the magnitude of their domestic needs; and the United States is not resigned to the emancipation of the European members of NATO. U.S. officials know that many of NATO's smaller powers are not unhappy at relying on the United States for their protection (and for paying for it), and that the UK, a recent convert to a common European defense, is still quite vulnerable to U.S. pressure and blandishments.

These are some of the key issues for Europe's future. They are sufficiently knotty to make progress laborious and slow. The uncertainties in Russia's future could also weigh heavily (and divisively) on the EU. However, at the beginning of the twenty-first century, there are reasons for optimism. Who would have predicted in 1945 that former mortal enemies would pool their sovereignty as extensively as they have, that the Franco-German antagonism would be succeeded by a highly effective *couple franco-allemand,* that the UK would begin to pull away from the special relationship with the United States that Churchill deemed vital? Much has been accomplished. The huge tasks that lie ahead are illuminated by Philippe de Schoutheete in this wise and far-sighted volume.

INTRODUCTION

Despite the number of publications, the mass of documents, and the avalanche of information on European affairs, it is often said that the public lacks points of reference, a sense of distance, and hence the perspective, the analytical categories, and the simple concepts that would enable it to judge them. This book is merely a modest effort, obviously subjective and partial, aimed at remedying that situation. It is an attempt to rationalize and present certain European debates by reference to a few basic concepts.

It has deliberately been kept brief in the hope that it will be read. Superficial, the expert might say, because this book is intended not for experts but for ordinary men and women who are interested in the European Union. For that same reason, it avoids acronyms, which belong to technocratic language, and footnotes, which belong to scholarly language. Readers will find references that may be of interest to them at the end of the book.

The aim here is not really to convince the reader. In my experience, one only ever convinces those who are already convinced. It is, however, intended to promote a better understanding of the Union, and perhaps to provoke thought, which is already a considerable ambition. It does not seek to be original. European affairs have been so frequently debated, reiterated, and rebuked that originality is an illusion.

Because the book lays no claim to originality, it contains numerous quotations. That is, first, a matter of honesty: to avoid giving the impression that I alone have discovered what others have produced before me. But the quotations are also intended to convey a certain sense of history. The European structure is not the recent fruit of the fastidious work of a handful of technocrats. It embodies a collective response, spanning a period of fifty years, to the challenges of the twentieth century. It is rooted in the history of our civilization: the history of events and the history of ideas. It reflects an element of political reality and an element of dream, but that dream is not idle fancy, as Alain Duhamel observes. The quotations are an attempt to demonstrate that continuity in time. In that respect, I would associate myself with Michel Eyquem de Montaigne: "It could be said of me that in this book I have only made up a bunch of other men's flowers, providing of my own only the string that binds them together."

Chapter 1

CONCEPT AND ACTION

*What has most distinguished men is that those who performed
great deeds perceived the extent to which they were possible before
others.*

—*Cardinal de Retz*

 The concept of Europe is rooted in history and mythology. For better and for worse! It was to some extent connected with the idea of "Christianity," which during the Middle Ages played a decisive civilizing and cultural role, while veiling the excesses of the Crusades or of the Inquisition. Later, it coincided more or less with the idea of "civilized nations," which underpinned the philosophy of Enlightenment, but which was also to provide an ideological basis for colonial expansion. In that abstract and distant form, the concept of European unity is now embedded in the subconscious of our nations as a common trunk of values, traditions, and history, which neither cultural diversity nor the bloodiest confrontations have been able to erase permanently, even in the paroxysm of conflicts, "The long history of what one might refer to as the call for Europe reflects the underlying idea that there is such a thing as a European 'common heritage'" (Millon-Delsol 1993).

That abstract and slightly mythical Europe was the Europe that

Charles de Gaulle presented in 1960 as being "the dream of the wise and the ambition of the powerful, which now appears to be the vital condition for equilibrium in the world." The territorial extent of that concept, and particularly its Eastern "limes," is not clearly perceived. Everything suggests that this perception is subjective: it varies according to the periods, the nations, and the individuals in question. It does, however, extend beyond the current territorial boundary of the European Union.

It would be wrong to claim that the venture launched in 1950 by Jean Monnet and Robert Schuman is entirely unconnected with that age-old concept, to which Aristide Briand, Gustav Stresemann, and Richard Coudenhove-Calgeri had given a new relevance between the two world wars. The Preamble of the Treaty of Paris, establishing the European Coal and Steel Community in 1951, refers to "a destiny henceforward shared." But the institutional framework that best reflects that common historical heritage is that of the Council of Europe. It is there that all European countries can meet, provided they satisfy the criteria of democracy and human rights that the group of member countries now considers as being the essential components of its fund of shared values. Those criteria are necessary. They are also sufficient. Countries wishing to become members of the Council of Europe are not required to participate in particular policies or make concessions in matters of sovereignty. They may ratify the numerous conventions, notably on legal and cultural matters, which the Council of Europe has very usefully drafted over the years, but they are under no obligation to do so. That has enabled the countries of Central and Eastern Europe, released from the Soviet yoke, to enter the Council of Europe without any particular difficulties or technical negotiations, and hence without delay. There they find confirmation of the historic fact that they belong to the European family, which nobody had ever disputed, even in the darkest hours. They also find recognition of, and to some extent the reward for, the silent and peaceful revolution that the restoration of democratic practices and the upholding of fundamental rights represents in those countries. Their membership in the Council of Europe confirms that they share with the other member countries a certain vision of humankind and of the fundamental elements of life in society, and hence a concept.

I n 1950, the Council of Europe did indeed embody that *concept,* as it does today: the European idea as drawn from the shared cultural heritage and from historical tradition. The proposals of Monnet and Schuman were novel, or different, in that they envisaged a structure aimed at *action,* and thus orientated toward the future. Of course, "Europe is both ancient and future" (Le Goff 1994), but the difference in approach remains fundamental.

It accounts for the fact, now somewhat forgotten, that it was *against* the Council of Europe, or at least by diverging from it, that the European Community was launched. That divergence related neither to ideas nor values. It related, and still relates, to methods, and the method was deemed to be essential. In the words of Monnet: "Those who failed to provide the method did not bring the problem closer to a solution."

Paul-Henri Spaak, who presided over three sessions of the Assembly of the Council of Europe between 1949 and 1951, resigned in December 1951 amid a certain fracas. One year earlier, he had supported Schuman's innovative initiative. On resigning, he explained his disappointment and discouragement vis-à-vis the practices of the Council of Europe in the following terms: "I was surprised at the amount of talent expended in that assembly in the process of explaining that it was necessary *not* to do something." He concluded thus: "We tried to find expressions of unanimity, which are expressions of impotence."

The Council of Europe does indeed take its decisions unanimously, with the help of an international secretariat, the role of which remains secondary. It is typical of a traditional model for international institutions, the classic example of which, even before World War II, was the League of Nations. This model has the significant advantage of providing optimum protection for the autonomy and independence of the states. It has the disadvantage of almost invariably operating inefficiently, which rapidly becomes a major hindrance whenever action is contemplated.

The European Community represents an entirely different model with no historical precedent, in which decisions usually involve a majority vote, and in which an institutional structure independent of the states (High Authority and Assembly, subsequently the European Commission and Parliament) plays an important role. That is the essential point. "Nothing is possible without men, nothing is lasting without institutions" (Monnet 1976).

That model inevitably implies a certain transfer of sovereignty by the states, which was not necessarily a frightening prospect for the more enlightened minds of the postwar political world. Winston Churchill wrote the following words to Stafford Cripps: "It is said with truth that this implies some sacrifice or merger of national sovereignty. But it is also possible and not less agreeable to regard it as a gradual assumption by all the nations concerned of that larger sovereignty which can also protect their diverse and distinctive customs and characteristics and their national traditions." In June 1950, Spaak's message was no different: "Let Mr. Schuman know that public opinion is with him, that it remains receptive to generous ideas and that it is willing, to a greater extent than one may believe, to support them, even at the expense of certain sacrifices."

To say that the Community model is more efficient than that of the Council of Europe is to state the obvious. One need only compare the respective contributions of each of those organizations during the past fifty years to the changes in European society, to its internal solidarity, and to its external influence. What distinguishes member states of the Community or of the Union from the other European states is not that the former are more European than the latter, more steeped in the shared values, or more pure in some way. It is that the former, in their concern for efficiency, and with a view to achieving a certain result—in other words through a shared ambition—have accepted a certain number of rules, limitations, and constraints that the others do not accept. The Community venture has grafted an action-orientated structure onto the enduring European concept.

There is nothing very original about the foregoing statement, but it opens the door to a number of other considerations.

Any venture based on a philosophy of action that introduces rules and constraints with a view to fulfilling shared ambitions is political by nature. To do that is the very essence of politics! In that perspective, the Community has been political from the outset, even though during its infancy it dealt only with coal and steel production. "A jumble of coal and steel has been proposed, with no idea of where it will lead, by reference to some form of industrial syndicate," said de Gaulle with contempt, eight days after Schuman's speech of 9 May 1950 launching the European Coal and Steel Community. Nevertheless, from the outset, although it was not even trying to deal with foreign policy or security matters, the venture was political on account of its aims and its method. Political through those factors alone, but genuinely political.

That was still the publicly proclaimed position of the signatories of the Treaty of Rome, despite the failure of the European Defense Community. In his memoirs, Spaak sought to describe the aspirations of his colleagues gathered at the Campidoglio:

> Full well did they measure the importance of the economic trans-formations they had just decided, but in their minds, those transfor-mations, for all their greatness, were merely accessory to, or, at the very least, the first stage of a yet greater political revolution.

It was only later, and particularly at the time of the successive enlargements, that European leaders presented the Community as an exclusively economic and commercial enterprise: a "common market" with no political scope. In so doing, some—no doubt with good intentions—assumed a heavy responsibility. The Danes and the British (perhaps others, too) can legitimately consider that they were deceived as to the merchandise in the political presentation of what was at stake, during the referendums, for example. With the passage of time, they see the Community or Union in a very different light. And that difference is no accident. From the outset, Europe was in fact different to what they were told. Many subsequent difficulties stem from that deliberate ambiguity. Even now, we are all still paying the price of it.

B ecause the venture is explicitly based on action or on the fulfillment of an ambition that, though not perceived by everyone at the same time in the same way, is nevertheless shared, it is normal that the efficiency criterion should be at the heart of the European debate. Indeed, we have seen how the issue of efficiency can arise at any moment, as in the discussions leading to the Single European Act, the Treaty of Maastricht, and the Treaty of Amsterdam. On the one hand, the efficiency that was shown in setting up the legislative framework for the internal market between 1987 and 1992 legitimized, a posteriori, the provisions of the Single European Act that enabled that framework to be created. On the other hand, the inefficiency perceived in matters of foreign policy, as in the case of Yugoslavia, in Bosnia or Kosovo, brings into question the operational provisions of the Maastricht Treaty in that domain and opens a debate on the political, institutional, and financial means required for a policy of that kind to see the light of day. The Amsterdam Treaty touches on that debate without, perhaps, finally settling it. As for inefficiency in the fight against unemployment, which is bitterly resented by public opinion, this would ultimately bring into question the legitimacy of the entire exercise.

At first sight, those judgments seem unfair: it is not Europe but the entire international community, all powers taken together, that has long remained powerless in Bosnia; and as for employment policy, it is not a matter for which the Community is principally responsible. Yet the general demand for efficiency is understandable. It is even legitimate and natural. Through several successive treaties the members of the Community have accepted binding and sometimes costly provisions, particularly with a view to gaining better collective control of their external environment and a thriving and socially equitable economy. In a sense, to the extent that they recognize the importance of the European structure, they have placed it under an obligation to achieve a certain result. "Government is a contrivance of human wisdom to provide for human wants. Men have a right that these wants should be provided for by this wisdom" (Burke 1790).

Efficiency is therefore one of the keys to the system. Any proposal in the European sphere has to be examined in the light of that criterion.

This analysis applies particularly to the issue of unanimity. In that respect, the following propositions appear, at first sight, to be purely common sense or practical experiences that each of us may have had in the various fields of professional or private life:

- The efficiency of any system depends largely on the way in which decisions are taken within it.
- A system in which decisions must be taken unanimously or by consensus is less efficient than one in which decisions are taken by a majority vote.
- That relative inefficiency grows in direct relation to the number of participants.
- The main reason why a system based on majority voting is more efficient is not that voting occurs frequently but simply that one is able to vote, which encourages each party to seek compromises; unanimity, in contrast, fuels intransigence, as each party knows that its own choice can suffice to block any decision.

The fact that those commonsense considerations also apply to European affairs has been demonstrated by the creation of the internal market. Once the Single European Act had introduced decision-making based on a qualified majority for almost all directives relating to the internal market (Article 95 of the European Community Treaty, Ex-article 100a), the latter was established within the stipulated deadline. A number of those directives had been blocked for more than a decade by the unanimity rule, which applied until the Single European Act came into force. However, most of the directives (approximately 220 out of 260), which under the Single

European Act could have been adopted by a qualified majority, were *in fact* unanimously approved. The members could have voted, but didn't! Which proves not only that the principle of decisionmaking by majority is an essential efficiency factor, but also that the application of that principle does not systematically create minorities among the members.

A further consideration that likewise reflects common sense and practical experience is that to be efficient, any decisionmaking system must be perceived as being equitable and proportionate to the issues at stake. Virtually all national constitutions, company by-laws, and internal rules of clubs and associations stipulate that some decisions, more important than others, can only be taken by a special majority.

The boundless imagination of lawyers has devised numerous majority voting systems. The "qualified majority" system favored by the authors of the Treaty of Rome is a compromise between the principle of "one state = one voice," which prevails in many of the traditional international organizations (such as the United Nations General Assembly and the Council of Europe), and the principle of attributing to each state a certain decisionmaking weight, proportionate to its size or contribution (as is the rule adopted by the International Monetary Fund, for example). The qualified majority gives more votes to large countries than to small countries, but that additional number of votes is not proportionate to the respective sizes of the countries.

This hybrid system, which reflects the hybrid nature of the institutional structure in which it operates, has generally been considered equitable in a Community containing roughly equal numbers of large and small states. As long as it applied essentially to the internal market and to the fundamental objectives of the Community, it was also perceived as being proportionate to the issues at stake. The acceptability of the system is evident in the fact that all parliaments of the Community ratified the Single European Act, which in 1985 considerably extended the use of a qualified majority. It is not surprising that this decisionmaking system is being reconsidered with the prospect of an enlarged Union containing many new states, most of which are small and dealing with other issues, particularly in external matters. That is, at least, a topic of discussion to which a rational approach can be adopted, taking into account the need for efficiency in decisionmaking, which is accepted in principle by all.

Sadly, the debate on this issue is far from being rational. It is being pursued with passion on the basis of a presentation divided into black and white, using imaginary and frequently surrealist examples, in terms that echo the sovereignty, independence, and vital interests of the member states. Obviously, no agreement will ever be reached on that basis. Should not the discussion be conducted on a more modest and pragmatic basis? Drawing on common sense and experience? Taking into account, above all, the vital interest of the Union, enlarged and endowed with a more extensive field of competence, in having an efficient decisionmaking procedure? Searching for application criteria that are perceived as being both equitable and proportionate to the issues at stake? On the whole, wherever genuine progress has been made in European affairs, it has been achieved through an approach of that kind.

Chapter 2

EMPIRE AND NATION

On the showing of Hellenic history we may expect that our present Western problem will receive its solution—in so far as it receives one at all—in some quarter or quarters where the institution of national sovereignty has not been erected into an object of idolatrous worship.

—*Arnold Toynbee*

 The process leading to European union is greatly hampered by a desire to apply existing political categories to the new political forms it seeks to create. That is, in particular, the case of those who wish to view the venture as creating an artificial and dominating political structure, disregarding cultural diversity and national identity: a multinational super-state or, in other words, an empire. The Carolingian or Lotharingian heritage of the six founder-states may account for the existence of that myth. The somewhat hackneyed expression "United States of Europe" has certainly sustained it by suggesting an unrealistic parallel with the U.S. melting pot.

The concept of an empire is badly viewed in Europe, and for good reason: most of the European nations were constituted against the more or less imperial ambitions of their neighbors. The first outline of a nation in France was sketched in the midst of conflict against the English during the Hundred Years' War; Spain grew out of the struggle against the Moors; Germany united against Napoleon; the Risorgimento in Italy occurred in response to foreign influence; and Belgium was formed in the balance between its neighbors' dominating ambitions. More recently, that imperial concept recurred in colonial expansion, which is the very expression of a will to dominate. Thus, to assimilate the construction of Europe with the building of an empire is a way of entering into a controversial debate. The image of an arrogant and imperial technocracy strikes a raw nerve. But the view is unfounded.

History confirms that empires share two characteristic features:

- They are established and maintained by force and deceit.
- They imply domination, by one or more nations, of other nations.

What of the Community and the Union?

Spaak, on signing the Treaty of Rome at the Campidoglio, was inspired by emotion; his contribution had been substantial. He spoke of "accomplishing the greatest voluntary and directed transformation of the history of Europe . . . whilst rejecting any use of force, any coercion and any threat, which is remarkable and perhaps unique." Nearly forty years later, Duhamel refers to an "audacious and ambitious answer to the logic of death and destruction which for too long had hounded the Old Continent."

The peaceful and peacemaking nature of the European integration process is in fact one of its principal traits and one of its main merits. It has achieved what forty years of communism, Soviet domination, and the KGB failed to achieve in Eastern Europe, that is, to settle the traditional antagonisms in a lasting way and to such an extent that a fratricidal war seems impossible. That result takes on its full significance if we consider the countless failures that preceded it: "There is nothing more lamentable than the history of the efforts that have been made, for centuries, to provide Western Europe with some permanent factor of order and peace: it is the tale of a series of failures" (Ganshof 1953).

Successive enlargements show that the Community has never ceased to attract new candidates, and sometimes in an embarrassing way. That attraction bears no sign of any force, deceit, or coercion; it simply demonstrates a will to participate in that "voluntary and directed transformation," that "audacious and ambitious answer." How could one explain that after so many years, so many candidates are asking to join, if the idea were to crush national identities and cultural diversity?

There is therefore no coercion. Neither is there any hegemony. That is a striking point. Most alliances, groupings, and international institutions contain a dominant power that, while observing certain rules, controls the game, leads the action, or exercises a pre-eminent role, whether in fact or law.

If we study closely the day-to-day operations of the European institutions, we can indeed discern subsystems within that whole, that is to say, lasting, systematic, and more or less formalized alliances that on a large range of subjects try to orient the action of the Union in a certain direction and are relatively successful in doing so. This applies to the Franco-German partnership, for example, and sometimes also to the Benelux countries. A southern solidarity unites several Mediterranean states, while the Nordic states share a Scandinavian solidarity. But there is nothing hegemonial in those relations. The temptation to establish a *directoire* of large states to determine the policy of the Community has existed, certainly in the case of General de Gaulle. Today, it is clearly still present in the minds of some leaders, and it is no doubt strengthened by the prospect of successive enlargements and by the Union's lack of effectiveness in foreign policy. However, if we examine the matter objectively, leaving aside dreams and fantasy, it seems that no significant initiative in the history of the Community can be attributed to the joint action of a *directoire* through which large states were able to impose their wishes on smaller states.

That fundamental point explains the attraction of the Union. Sweden, Finland, and Austria wanted to join because they could see that other similarly sized states felt at ease within the Union and were genuinely involved in the decisionmaking process. The countries of Central and Eastern Europe, which were subjected to an imposed, dominant, and oppressive structure for forty years, now turn to the European Union precisely because it is none of those things. They have experienced an empire and no longer want one; they are attracted to the Union because it has no imperial quality. Delors has said of the Community that it represents "the longest experience of managing interdependencies in a common framework and without hegemony from any nation."

That absence of hegemony is essentially due to the institutional structure proposed by Monnet and Schuman. It was designed to be independent of the member states, hence the central role of initiation and management conferred on the High Authority of the Coal and Steel Community and subsequently on the Commission. It was designed to be efficient, hence the introduction of majority voting. It was designed to operate under rules of law that were equal for all, hence the role attributed to the Court of Justice. The structure's characteristic independence, efficiency, and emphasis on law constitutes an advantage for all participants, but the advantage is greater for the less powerful. In international life, as in the daily life of individuals, the proper functioning of institutions, their independence, and their observance of the law protect the weak above all. The strong can hope to defend themselves alone, sometimes by crushing their neighbors.

In a book entitled *Making Sense of Europe* (which expresses a fine ambition!), Christopher Tugendhat, a former British member of the European Commission who is now chairman of the Royal Institute of International Affairs in London, expresses that idea as follows:

It is the fate of small and relatively weak countries to be trampled on when their large neighbours make war and to have their interests squeezed when these neighbours make up. . . . The beauty of the Schuman and subsequent proposals was that they held out the prospect of guarantees of equality undreamt of in previous attempts at European co-operation.

To enshrine that nonhegemonial quality and secure the participation of the Benelux countries in the common enterprise—participation that was deemed essential from the start—those countries were given a place within the institutions, and thus an influence that was disproportionate to their size. This applies to the members of the Commission, the number of members of Parliament, and the weight of the votes in the Council. "The voting rules within the Council are such that there is no diktat, no preponderance" (Hallstein). These arrangements were precisely intended to reassure the three countries concerned, to demonstrate that the idea was not to subject them to an individual or collective dominating enterprise, or to an empire under construction.

That initial concession was extended to new member states of similar size. Now that the prospect of further enlargements looms, it is being called into question, at least partially. That is easily explained. Nearly all of the countries concerned by those future enlargements are considered to be small, and consequently the numerical balance between large and small countries is likely to be upset. That is an accidental fact, but it means that for the first time in the history of the Community a certain antagonism has emerged between large and small partners. This was evident during the negotiation of the Treaty of Amsterdam. To defuse that antagonism, which is dangerous for the future, various ideas are being considered, such as altering the initial proportions or adding a population criterion to the weighting of the votes. All proposals are worth considering, but wisdom and common sense dictate that the fundamental feature of the system should remain intact, namely, the absence of any individual or collective domination within the Union, or in other words, the absence of hegemony.

The European Union, such as it has developed over the past forty years, is not imperial. There is no "European plot" against nations, as some critics would have us believe. The venture presents no threat to the nations participating in it. On the contrary, its partisans would say that it adds to their standing. It does not threaten them because its object is not to create a new state that would somehow mysteriously substitute itself for the states we know. Its object is to create a different, complex, and innovative structure. "Europe must now invent a form of unity other than that of an empire" (Le Goff 1994). That structure cannot be analyzed by reference to traditional public law categories, because those categories, which were devised to describe the organization of states, cannot be transposed to describe something fundamentally different. "The Community on which the Union is founded represents a model which differs radically from all past or present federations" (Duverger 1994). That is why the debate on the idea of a federal Europe has always proved so sterile.

The truth is that the concept of federalism, though fairly clear to lawyers, is politically ambiguous within the Union, because it brings to mind different reference models. In Continental Europe, the model that will most readily spring to mind is that of federal Germany, which is a model of *decentralization* after Adolf Hitler's authoritarian regime. In Britain, the most obvious model will be that of the United States, which is a model of *centralization* after the Union fought against the Confederates in the Civil War. These implicit connotations, which are different and even opposite, would be sufficient, by themselves, to complicate the issue.

In addition, the actual concept of a federal state was shaped by political scientists, in the context of the theory of states, to describe one of the forms in which power may be exercised within a state structure. In the case of the European Union, the idea is not to create a state, and the concept is therefore not directly applicable. One can of course say that some aspects of the Community machine have been inspired by federalism, just as other aspects bear the hallmark of confederalism. Valéry Giscard d'Estaing refers legitimately to a "confederation under partly federative management." Likewise, we may want the Union to have "a federal vocation," as suggested in the draft text initially submitted to the European Council at Maastricht. These are comparisons, or approximations, that seek to categorize a complex and ambiguous reality using the limited number of concepts that exist to describe the decisionmaking process operating in a public law entity. But the Community, such as it has developed over the past decades, is neither a traditional international organization nor a nascent state. As Monnet said with great simplicity, it is "a new political form."

Although the European structure threatens neither the existence of the states nor the identity of the nations participating in it, it nevertheless makes certain demands.

It implies that a multinational European entity should be able to play a role of its own on the international stage. That is what was unacceptable to General de Gaulle, who considered that "states are the only entities which have the right to order and the power to be obeyed" (de Gaulle 1970). He gave this explanation to André Malraux: "As for Europe, you know as well as I do that it will be either an agreement between States, or nothing. Therefore: nothing" (Malraux 1976). That argument has aged. Today's European Union is not nothing. Neither is it merely an agreement between states. Who would dispute that the Community in its own right plays a significant role in international life, and that within its own sphere of competence (competition, for example) it orders and is obeyed?

In the past, states were considered to be masters of space and time. Space meant national boundaries, and time meant the policies pursued within those boundaries. That view no longer reflects reality. "The vision of a State as master within its own territory, legislating independently, is doubly redundant: the borders are open and the limits imposed on legislation are far more strict than was previously the case" (Thibaud 1995).

The European integration process also implies that participating states should reject the ideology of nationalism, or, in the words of Toynbee, that they should not erect the institution of national sovereignty into an object of idolatrous worship. "The way in which each state defines its national interest is not universally identical, but is founded on a pre-existing ideological base" (Fukuyama 1989). Monnet's aim was precisely to persuade the states of Western Europe to define their interests by reference to a nonnationalist ideological base. That accounts for his success in a continent that had suffered the bloodiest experience of nationalist ideology. It also accounts for the fact that, even now, European ambitions are liable to clash with small- or large-scale nationalism arising, or resurfacing, here and there.

Indeed, that ideology is always ready to resurface. There are signs of it in the countries recently freed from the Soviet yoke, and that is understandable.

> Poland will have to make the choice that we made during the fifties, which is to transfer part of its decisionmaking power, in other words its sovereignty, to a supranational level. That is a difficult choice to make. Even more difficult, perhaps, for countries which have only recently regained full sovereignty; but it is an essential choice without which there can be no strong Europe. (Dehaene 1995)

"Nationalism is war," said François Mitterand in his last speech to the European Parliament. Helmut Kohl echoed his words, declaring that "the policy of European integration really boils down to the question of war or peace for the twenty-first century." Ideology is at stake, not the nation or the state.

Western Europe invented the concept of the nation-state and spread it throughout the world during the past two centuries. Taken to the extreme, it implies a single and exclusive allegiance between the citizen and the state of which the citizen is a national. All nationalism is based on that exclusive single bond. However, history demonstrates that a single allegiance of that kind does not reflect reality. The historical situation is one of multiple allegiances to town and region, to province or kingdom, to a dynasty, a language, or a religion. According to place and time, they are combined, cumulated,

20

or superposed; they precede, accompany, or replace national allegiance. Each one in turn may be dominant. The authors of a recent atlas of Western European nations note: "No simple geographical delimitation could convey a reality which, now as always, involves layering and interlocking." From that point of view, the European Union, and the network surrounding it, is merely an interlocking part among others—neither exclusive nor destructive, but the reflection of a complex reality.

Chapter 3

STRUCTURE AND NETWORK

It is only by chance that one sees precisely that which one cares not to observe.

—*Jean-Jacques Rousseau*

 Few people are willing to view the European Union as it is. It has its vices and virtues, its qualities and faults, its strengths and weaknesses. But all of these are hard to discern through the complexity of the texts and procedures.

In reality, the sketch that lies before us is plainly unfinished. It has been assembled gradually through a series of touch-ups. It is the product of an evolution in which one can certainly perceive a guiding line but also a fair number of detours, inconsistencies, and areas of ambiguity or ambivalence—in the Maastricht and Amsterdam Treaties, for example. In that respect, the Union reflects the uncertainties and disagreements of its member states. What could be more normal?

Whenever the Union is presented, we usually find that either its defects or its qualities have been omitted from the presentation. When its cohesion is emphasized, the Union becomes threatening. When its incoherence is highlighted, it seems ridiculous. Some describe the Union as they would like it to be, while others describe it as they fear it might eventually become: a mythical and unreal Europe. "They believe not that which is but that which they see, and they see not that which is but that which they believe" (Duhamel 1995).

A well-informed but realistic and unprejudiced observer contemplating the European structure for the first time would no doubt be struck initially by its extreme originality. The structure is original in many respects, but three features in particular would be likely to capture the observer's attention:

1. Areas of *exclusive competence* are transferred definitively and by treaty to the common organization, meaning, among other things, that individual member states can no longer enter into commercial agreements with nonmember states and that they are no longer entitled to determine among themselves the residence rights of their nationals.

2. The structure is a *lawmaking* structure, generating rules that are binding on the legislature of each member state, take precedence over national law, and can apply directly to citizens.

3. *International personality*, or, in legal terms, the right of active and passive legation, accounts for the fact that one of the planet's largest diplomatic corps is accredited to the Union and that its own ambassadors are received as such in most of the world's capitals.

No international entity, other than states, has possessed all of those characteristics simultaneously at any time in history. Thus, the structure is genuinely and profoundly original. That does not make the European Union a state, but although it cannot be treated as the exact equivalent of a state, neither can it be put in the same category as other international organizations. It is different in nature.

T he cause or consequence (both arguments are valid) of that originality in nature and substance lies in the fact that the institutional structure also is original. No international organization other than the European Community has, in addition to the Council in which the states have their seats:

- a multinational, directly elected Parliament;
- an institution independent of the states with a monopoly on initiating legislation, namely, the Commission;
- and a Court of Justice generating case law that is binding on all courts.

Leaving aside the judicial function, which, as in all other cases, is exercised by a Court, the relations within the institutional triangle—Parliament, Council, Commission—are at the heart of the Community system. This system is original in so far as it seeks equilibrium not through the separation of powers, as in most European constitutions, but in the division of competence. That is what constitutes the Community method, "which results from organised dialogue between the member States and the common institutions, exercising together a delegated sovereignty" (Fontaine 1990).

In the *legislative* field—and there must be legislation because the Community is a lawmaking structure—most of the power is held by the Council, in other words, by the states. Directives or regulations can be adopted against the wishes of the Commission and even against a majority of the Parliament (except in the yet limited number of cases to which the co-decision procedure applies), but they can never be adopted without at least a qualified majority of the Council. That power vested in the Council is tempered by the monopoly granted to the Commission, as the organ representing the collective interest, over the initiation of legislation; the Council can only disregard such initiatives by a unanimous decision. It is also tempered by the role given to the Parliament, which extends from mere consultation to genuine co-decision, with various intermediate options, now so numerous and complex that they contribute to the unintelligibility of the system.

As far as the *executive* is concerned, in the Community field *stricto sensu* (the First Pillar of Maastricht), the Commission is the focal point. It monitors compliance with the treaty and with the law

25

derived from it, such as the 280 directives framing the internal market. It also provides external representation. For example, from 1986 to 1993, during the Uruguay Round, it negotiated the agreements that founded the World Trade Organization. In exercising those functions, the Commission is supervised on two levels, by the Council and by the Parliament. Supervision by the Council usually takes the form of committees of national civil servants monitoring the activities of the Commission and operating under a variety of different and complex rules ("commitology") that add to the obscurity of the system. The Parliament supervises primarily through its budgetary power, which it uses extensively and sometimes even abuses, when it tries to interfere in day-to-day policy management.

In the specific fields of external policy, security, home affairs, and justice (the Second and Third Pillars of Maastricht), most of the executive power is vested in the Council.

The initial structure has developed over the years with the creation of new bodies such as the Court of Auditors, the Court of First Instances, and the Committee of the Regions. Decentralization has been achieved by the creation of specialized agencies, particularly in the fields of trademarks and patents, the environment, pharmaceuticals, and police. A large number of committees of senior civil servants of member states have gradually been constituted and often play a decisive role in defining policies concerning agriculture, currency, external trade, employment, foreign policy, police, and justice. The oldest of those committees, the Committee of Permanent Representatives, with the assistance of roughly 100 working groups, endeavors to prepare in a coherent manner the ministerial sessions of the Council, which meet in some twenty different formations: ministers of foreign affairs, finance, agriculture, transport, education, social affairs, budget, and many others.

At the summit, the biannual meetings of heads of state and of government—the European Council—top the pyramid.

That machinery as a whole is supported by an administration that is fairly large, though not as excessive as is said: more than 15,000 employees for the Commission, approximately 3,500 for the Parliament, 2,500 for the Council, and less than 1,000 for the Court of Justice. At least one-third of those employees work in the translation and interpreting departments, the size of which is due to the fact that there are now eleven official languages.

The structure as a whole is striking in its size, in the variety of the subjects it deals with, in its constant growth, its endurance, and its cohesion. This creates a fear of excessive centralization. The structure obviously owes its efficiency to its originality; but the fact that it is unusual also accounts for the fears it generates. The debate over the ratification of the Maastricht Treaty was shadowed by the image of a monolithic, centralizing, finicky, arrogant, and bureaucratic bloc, gradually invading the sphere of autonomy of both states and individuals. The Treaty of Amsterdam has not dispelled those fantasies. Nevertheless, as a result of its history, the structure is heterogeneous and fragmented and therefore much more flexible than it appears to be on first sight.

I n its early years, from 1950 to 1955, the European structure developed according to an extremely coherent design. The idea was to extend the Community method and the institutional structure initially conceived by Jean Monnet for the Coal and Steel Community, little by little, to all subjects of common interest. That was the ambition behind the European Defense Community and the European Political Community projects. Some observers still cling to the somewhat nostalgic hope of one day restoring that single and coherent approach, which was both efficient and intellectually satisfactory.

However, after the failure of the European Defense Community in 1955, and without abandoning the *acquis communautaire* (Community laws, practices, principles, and objectives), Europe embarked on other, slightly different courses. The leaders sought and often found acceptable solutions to specific problems. Those solutions were sometimes close to the initial design, but sometimes far from it. Even for the most ardent supporters, the idea was to create not an ideal Europe but a possible Europe. To achieve that, at each stage the challenges of the moment had to be tackled with "realistic and workable proposals," to quote the phrase used in the 1975 Tindemans report.

The passage of time, institutional practice, a number of improvisations, and changes in mentality then shaped the structure. The result as we see it today bears the mark of its history. It is heterogeneous, unequally structured, and based on texts that are sometimes ambiguous or contradictory. Its form is not that of a hierarchy but of a diversified network that has gradually woven itself around the institutional center provided by the European Community. Let us examine that network.

First, we find intergovernmental cooperation, which took shape from 1970 onward in the field of external policy (under the name of "political cooperation"), and from 1976 onward in the field of justice and home affairs (under the name "Trevi cooperation"). These new forms, which were gradually extended, deepened, and made systematic, undoubtedly helped to create a certain political image of Europe, both internally and externally. The original intention was that these matters should remain entirely separate from the activities of the Community, for they were based on a principle of cooperation rather than integration. Initially, the institutions of the Treaty of Rome played only a minor role in them. For many years, vigilant watchdogs ensured that this barrier, which was supposed to separate different visions of the European process, remained in place.

As time passed, a pragmatic approach, internal logic, and the concern for efficiency attenuated those initial differences. Eventually, it was admitted by all that the distinction was sometimes artificial and that the dividing line was blurred. From then on, the role of the Community institutions grew progressively.

The culmination, or at least the provisional culmination, of that development is to be found in the Treaty of Maastricht, which turns those two long-standing areas of cooperation into two separate pillars of the Union (Titles V and VI of the EU treaty), while providing for a "single institutional framework" (Article 3 of the EU treaty, Ex-article C) within which to debate, under various procedures, all policies of the Union. Nevertheless, the principle of separation is reaffirmed. These pillars are connected to the Community machinery and operate within the same framework, but they are not part of it. They are the first link in a network, *close* to the center but not quite *in* the center. The Treaty of Amsterdam does not really review that ambiguous situation, despite the existence of a number of genuine difficulties regarding the day-to-day application of the Maastricht Treaty within the Union. The Treaty of Amsterdam alters the boundaries between the various pillars and shifts some subjects from one pillar to another, but the principle of that separation remains fixed.

Moving on to the protocol on social policy attached to the Maastricht Treaty, we find ourselves in a slightly different case. This is not quite a Community norm, for one member state is missing: the United Kingdom, which initially refused to sign the protocol. It was therefore necessary to change the decisionmaking procedure so as to take into account that absence. In that way, and wrongly no doubt, a legal basis was given to a "social" Europe with a different composition and different procedures to those of the treaty. This solution, which was unfortunate from the outset, also proved difficult to implement in practice. A change of mind in the United Kingdom enabled the social protocol to be introduced, through the Treaty of Amsterdam, into the common law of the Community. But that same treaty, by incorporating the Schengen agreements to permit free movement of persons and control of external borders, has created a particular legal situation, since these new provisions do not apply to the United Kingdom or to Ireland. In this area, we find a further aspect of the network, close to the center but not quite in the center.

Because monetary union initially concerns only some of the member states, we have here a further case, similar to the previous one, in which a fundamental Union policy operates with a particular composition and under specific procedures.

The way in which the treaty provides for organizations that existed before the Community, such as Benelux or the Western European Union, is worth considering in this context. They operate under their own rules. The states that are members of those organizations are not the same group as those that form the European Union. The Community institutions play no role in them. Nevertheless, the treaty recognizes their existence and, in the case of the Western European Union, even gives it a certain function: to "elaborate and implement decisions and actions of the Union which have defence implications." Within the European structure, these organizations constitute subsystems, additional links in a network of relations spreading gradually from the center outward.

The "call" for European initiatives has also given rise at regular intervals to particular forms of intergovernmental cooperation involving certain member states. This occurred, for example, with the Schengen agreements. It also occurred in the military domain, with the agreements that led to the creation of the Eurocorps. Initially, those initiatives have no connection or only a slight connection with the Community machinery, although the Commission does attend the Schengen meetings, for example. However, their aims are those of the treaty, or are very close to them. Consequently, they tend to gravitate around the central core, and if circumstances are favorable, it is envisaged that they should eventually be incorporated into or at least legally connected to the core in some way. The incorporation of the Schengen agreements was the subject of delicate negotiations during the intergovernmental conference that led to the Treaty of Amsterdam. The solutions that were adopted lack clarity, and they are now proving difficult to apply in practice. But whatever their connection with the Union may be, these various forms of cooperation are in any case part of the network.

Moving from the center toward the periphery, we find other organizations that are more or less centered on the Union without quite belonging within its framework. This applies to the "Eureka" structures set up from 1985 onward in the field of applied research and later in the audiovisual sector. The Community institutions are present and play an important role in them. These organizations form part of the European network but are not part of the Union. A geographical extension of the network has resulted from association with the countries belonging to the European Free Trade Association, in the context of the European Economic Area. The treaty creating that area, which was signed in 1992, gives an important role to the Community institutions, including the Commission and the Court. But once again, we are not *in* the Union.

Detailed analysis yields numerous examples. What is the status of the Franco-German cooperation, formalized in 1963 by the Elysée Treaty? It is not part of the Union, but its role in the dynamics of Europe is universally recognized. It is obviously part of the network. What of the agreements signed with countries wishing to join the Union? For several years, we have pursued a structured dialogue with those countries of Central and Eastern Europe involving frequent meetings on several levels, including the ministerial level. Is that not an extension of the network? The truth is that the institutional variations surrounding the Community core are countless.

One also has to consider that on the fringe of all those structures, though not unconnected with them, there is a whole nebula of federations, representations, syndicates, professional or regional interest groupings, and associations of various kinds gravitating in the orbit of the Community institutions. They, too, form part of the network. Indeed, their actual raison d'être is to seek to penetrate the network.

The fact that Europe is not only a strong and coherent institutional structure but also, and perhaps above all, a multiform network of procedures and heterogeneous constructions providing flexible answers to differing needs, is not clearly perceived by public opinion. To most journalists and their readers, who also constitute the electorate, that whole cluster is "Brussels." And Brussels, by definition, is centralizing, bureaucratic, and arrogant. Obviously, simple ideas prevail over complex reality; the reassuring myth over objective analysis; the imaginary over the truth.

However, that reality is firmly grasped by political analysts who agree to a remarkable extent in their assessment of the Community phenomenon. "The Community of the Eighties is a complex whole in which more or less tightly-woven networks of integration and cooperation overlap one another" (Moreau-Desfarges 1985). Indeed, what Maastricht establishes is a set of different procedures, some of integration, others of cooperation. One can speak of a "Community system," gathering together around the institution's various "associated structures" and networks of intergovernmental cooperation (Wallace 1990). Stanley Hoffmann, a professor at Harvard and undoubtedly one of the foremost American observers of European affairs, has written: "The Community political system can best be visualized as an elaborate set of networks, closely linked in some ways, partially decomposed in others." Another American author refers to a "partial polity" and to "segmented federalism" (Sbragia 1992).

But it is one of the characteristic features of that network to be centered on the Community. The two new pillars of the Union are defined in relation to the first. The other institutions, the subsystems, the groupings and regroupings, formal or informal, gravitate about that pole. "European legitimacy is held by the Community, the institutions of which constitute the hard core, or the axis of unification" (Moreau-Desfarges 1985). Borrowing an image from Fernand Braudel, one might say that the Union is a "whole with multiple areas of cohesion."

This gradual development of a European organic network may be the beginnings of a new world: "The dispute between nationalists and federalists is a confrontation between two institutional visions, in which the reflexes of a vanishing world are revealing their inability to encompass the new world that is beginning" (Guéhenno 1993). Europe ought not to immobilize itself within an institutional structure but should remain an open system reflecting no clear-cut architecture and participating worldwide in an "aggregate of networks, linked amongst themselves like the inter-linked circles that symbolise the Olympic games" (Guéhenno 1993).

The fact remains that this "open system in an eminently fluid world" is not very intelligible. "How can one envisage an entangled, interdependent world without the sovereignty of nations losing all reality" (Thibaud 1995)? That world is difficult to describe and to explain. It has no emotive value. It arouses neither enthusiasm nor a spirit of sacrifice, or at least not while it has no clear objective justifying it all. But neither can one say that it is monolithic and centralizing, dominating and arrogant. It is far too diverse for that.

Chapter 4

LAW AND POLITICS

Which is more necessary to a society of weak men united through their weakness: gentleness or austerity? Both must be used: let the law be harsh and men indulgent.

—*Marquis de Vauvenargues*

 From the outset, the Community has been strongly marked by law, and particularly by the French legal tradition that fielded Pierre Uri, "one of the main architects of the Treaty of Rome," as Spaak observed. Legal argument is omnipresent in internal debate at all levels, in all institutions, and between those institutions.

That legal approach to problems is what newcomers to Community life are most struck by. It explains the important role played by decisions of the Court of Justice in the development of the Community. In a world where any difference of opinion takes a legal turn, he who "states the law" necessarily has a major role.

In a sense, the importance of law in the daily life of the European institutions reflects the primary vocation of the Community. Conflicts of opinion or interest between member states are now resolved neither by armed force nor, principally, by economic pressure, but by a rule of law accepted by all and interpreted by

33

the Court of Justice. In relations between member states, the ultima ratio regis is no longer the cannon but the treaty. From the point of view of civilization, that represents definite progress!

That progress is beneficial to all, but more so to the small than to the large. In international life as indeed elsewhere, the weaker a nation is, the greater its interest in having conflicts resolved by law rather than by force or by the interplay of influential pressure. That explains why the three Benelux countries have always been particularly attached to the European institutional system. Like other states, they have their differences on specific issues with the Commission or with the Parliament. Sometimes they are even condemned by the Court (more often than in turn as far as Belgium is concerned) for contravening Community law. As a matter of principle, however, they are attached to the prerogatives of the Commission, to the rights of the Parliament, and to the jurisdiction of the Court. Those issues were at the center of their concerns at the successive intergovernmental conferences that modified the treaty. They can be found in the position that the Benelux countries themselves defined on the eve of the Turin conference, which in March 1996 launched new negotiations. It is obviously very much in the interest of those countries to maintain a strong institutional structure and the predominance of law. But ultimately, is that interest not shared by all of the member states?

Two fundamental principles form the basis of Community law and distinguish it from ordinary international law. The first principle is the direct effect of Community law; in other words, Community law in itself creates rights and obligations for individuals. The second is that Community law prevails over national law.

Those principles do not appear explicitly in the treaty, but they were inferred from the treaty, in 1964, in a leading judgment of the Court of Justice. The Court held that "by contrast with ordinary international treaties, the EEC treaty created its own legal system, which, on the entry into force of the treaty, became an integral part of the legal system of the member States and which their courts are bound to apply." That is the principle of the primacy of European law. The Court went on to state that by the treaty, the member states "created a body of law which binds both their nationals and themselves." That is the direct effect.

The influence that the Court's case law has exerted and continues to exert on the development of the European structure has been criticized, particularly by those who favor intergovernmental structures. Some commentators have referred to "usurpation by the Court of Luxembourg, when it transforms declarations of political intentions into rules of law" (Thibaud 1995). Yet one can hardly dispute that the primacy of European law is the logical and inevitable consequence of the transfer, on the European level, of the power to enact laws in certain spheres (the internal market, for example). It would be impossible, without creating chaos, to transfer that legislative power to the Community while allowing the states to retain the power to enact divergent or contradictory laws. Luxembourg's Judge Pierre Pescatore, who was an influential member of the Court in its early years, wrote: "Any challenge to the principle of the primacy of Community law would bring into question the very existence of the Community."

The case law of the Court of Justice concerning the primacy and direct effect of Community law has been adopted by the supreme courts of all member states. In 1971, the Belgian Supreme Court ruled that "the judge must exclude the application of provisions of internal law which are contrary to a provision of the Treaty." In 1975, the Paris Court of Appeal, followed by the French Supreme Court, confirmed that "the provisions of the Treaty of Rome take precedence over [national] legislative provisions, including those enacted after the Treaty of Rome." Similar rulings were made by the Constitutional Court of Karlsruhe in 1971 and by the Italian Constitutional Court and the British High Court in 1973. The French Conseil d'État, having long remained reticent, finally endorsed that case law in 1989 and 1990.

Thus, the European Court of Justice is not simply stating a principle of law in isolation; all of the supreme courts of the member states consider that the Community constitutes a legal order in its own right. They therefore recognize the primacy of European law. In so doing, they emphasize the importance of the rule of law in Community life.

The power of Community law, its infiltration into the daily life of the member states, represents one of the strengths of the Community. That factor distinguishes the Community substantially from other international organizations. It also renders it more resistant to attacks and whims, more lasting, more profoundly rooted, and closer to the citizens, who can invoke the provisions of Community law directly. "Unlike international treaties of the normal type, the Community treaties grant individuals rights which the national courts must protect" (Isaac 1994).

The importance that Community law can assume in daily life and in protecting the rights of individuals emerged vividly in the judgment rendered by the Court on 15 December 1995 in the Jean-Marc Bosman case. Bosman, a footballer playing for the Racing Club of Liège, felt that his rights had been infringed and his career compromised by the traditional and previously unchallenged practice of "indemnities" paid by one club to another for the transfer of a professional player. He was unable to transfer from Liège to Dunkerque, despite the latter club's agreement to hire him, because the two clubs could not agree on the indemnity that one club was to pay to the other. At the end of a lengthy and highly publicized legal battle, the Court of Justice ruled that it was contrary to European law that a professional player from a member state should only be able to be employed by a club of another member state on condition that the latter club first paid a "transfer indemnity" to the previous employer. Thus, Bosman won his case against his former club, which had been actively supported not only by the Belgian football federation but also by the European federation. An individual footballer triumphed against the all-powerful system of European football! Since that judgment, the entire sporting world has been obliged to change its practices.

Although Community law can be important in the life of individuals, as that example demonstrates, it obviously enters into all aspects of the life of the institutions. However, the life of the institutions is not confined to legal debate. Politics are always present, and it is the interaction, and sometimes the interference, between law and politics that sets the rhythm of European debates.

One of the first conflicts between law and politics in the Community occurred during the 1965 crisis that culminated in what is wrongly referred to as the "Luxembourg Compromise." When they gathered in Luxembourg in January 1966, the foreign ministers of the six founding member states were confronted with two problems:

1. The treaty stipulated that from 1 January 1966, a series of decisions, particularly on agricultural matters, could take effect if approved by a qualified majority.
2. The French government, irritated by what it considered as the Commission's arrogant attitude, was disputing that prospect, despite the wording of the treaty, and had abandoned its seat on the Council for six months.

The compromise, which was largely attributable to Spaak and to Maurice Couve de Murville, really amounted to a statement of disagreement. Where "very important interests" were at stake (the expression usually mentioned today is "vital interests"), the six member states agreed that it was necessary to try to find a solution acceptable to all within a reasonable period of time. France alone considered that "the discussion must continue until a unanimous agreement is reached," which in this case implied it would not accept a majority decision. In practice, that attitude, which the United Kingdom and Denmark shared on ratifying the treaty, inhibited the use of majority voting for many years, except in determining the Community's annual budget. Each member feared that it would cause a political crisis by demanding a vote, even in cases where the treaty authorized voting. By extending the use of qualified majorities, particularly for the purposes of the internal market, the Single European Act enabled them to overcome that fear.

Whatever legal rule is involved, it is obvious that the collective interest of the Community cannot be served by a decision threatening a vital interest of a member state. That is not a matter of majority but one of common sense: it represents the principle of legitimate defense transposed to the Community level. The difficulty arises in seeking to establish *who* should determine the existence of such an interest. What is vital?

Germany and Italy, which had initially refused to accept France's position in the Luxembourg Compromise, have nevertheless relied on it once at the Council of Ministers for Agriculture. For Germany, the issue was that of fixing the annual price of wheat. For Italy, it was an import quota on oranges. These issues were certainly important. But were they vital?

The members of the Council, who are politicians, are receptive to the political arguments of their colleagues. Each of them knows that he or she, too, may one day face difficulty in a particular case—hence the exceptions, exemptions, compensations, and declarations that surround so many of the Council's decisions. In their own way, with the agreement of all parties, those decisions take into account the particular interests of one member state or another.

It is one thing to search, sometimes at length, for arrangements and compromises, but quite another to grant a member state the right to be its own sole judge and to block a decision, perhaps arbitrarily. Everyone accepts that a motorist may breach the highway code in order to save a life; but that the motorist should be sole judge of the reasons for his or her actions is not possible and would lead to anarchy. If it were applied regularly, the Luxembourg Compromise would bring the Community to a standstill in the often illusory search for consensus.

That no doubt accounts for the fact that it is rarely used. Indeed, during the past few years, it has not been used at all. Everyone knows that it is a dangerous weapon, especially in an enlarged Community. It is also double-edged, because one country may have a major interest in reaching a decision but another country a major interest in preventing one. That could have been the case, for example, in the difficult and repetitive debates surrounding the end of the negotiation of the Uruguay Round in autumn 1993. Since it was dealing with trade policy, the Council could in principle decide by a qualified majority. France, which was not satisfied with the results, denounced the agreements reached between the Commission and the United States at Blair House, threatened to block everything, and referred to its vital interest. Everyone grasped the message, not least the Belgian presidency. But Germany and Great Britain had a vital interest in bringing those lengthy negotiations, which were essential for world trade, to their conclusion. Thankfully, the Luxembourg Compromise was not invoked. An arrangement satisfying all parties was reached during the last weeks of the year. Referring to those events, Maurice Duverger described the French strategy as being one of "yes via no": refuse firmly at first, so as to be able later to accept a variation on the initial proposal. Very good! But what if another country were to resort to a strategy of "no via no"?

That so-called right to veto, which is not provided for in the treaty, introduces a risk of arbitrariness into a legal system. Fiercely defended in principle by some countries, it is seldom or never used in practice. Its weight is purely political, and that weight is limited. It is difficult to wield, and hence far less important than its supporters believe. It is, however, an element that cannot be entirely ignored in the complex equation that describes the decisionmaking process within the Union.

F or half a century, the member states have recognized that they have a superior political interest in pursuing the European integration process. If that were not the case, why would they belong to the Union? To that end, they have provided themselves with an efficient institutional machine and an elaborate legal structure, which they accept as being binding on them. But the fact remains that those elements are underpinned by implicit, underlying political agreements of fundamental importance.

One of those agreements involved giving the smaller countries of the initial Community a weight within the institutions that was disproportionate to their size, in order to secure their participation in the common venture. Even today, that is what gives the Community its nonhegemonial quality. This is discussed elsewhere.

Another agreement involved combining the opening of the common market for industrial products with the implementation of a policy aimed at supporting agricultural production. In this case, the agreement was initially Franco-German. As early as 1958, de Gaulle discussed with Konrad Adenauer the "problem of agriculture, to which France needs a solution." It was initially thought that the benefits German industry would gain from the opening of its neighbors' markets would in a sense be compensated by those that French agriculture would derive from a common policy. The reality proved more complex, but the common agricultural policy, for all the criticism it receives, remains one of the pillars of the Community.

A third agreement of that type is implicitly included in the ratification treaties of Spain and Portugal. Those treaties obviously represent the incorporation into the European structure of countries that had long been marginalized by their history. But they also involve opening up long-protected markets and thereby expanding the Community's internal market in return for a policy of cohesion, backed up by substantial financial aid for the new members, in the form of the Community's structural funds.

These agreements, like others that could be identified in fields such as fishing, research, trade policy, regional policy, or currency, share a common feature in that they are all expressions of internal solidarity: between large and small, town and country, center and periphery, north and south. As such, they constitute a cement within the Union—the political substratum on which the institutional structure and legal machinery that form the most visible part of the European edifice have been built.

Those tacit agreements are not necessarily eternal. Their principles or the way in which they operate may be brought into question as circumstances evolve. Here, as elsewhere, the future enlargement of the Union is raising questions as to the continuation of old agreements and the appearance of new ones. But those who bring the past into question must not lose sight, as some appear to do, of the historical, political, and psychological importance of those implied contracts, those points of balance in the life of the Community. In any case, their existence demonstrates that although the rule of law is essential to the Union, it is not the structure's only source of strength. Law and politics mingle and are mutually supportive.

Chapter 5

SUBSIDIARITY AND INTERVENTION

The legitimate object of government is to do for a community of people whatever they need to have done but cannot do at all or cannot so well do for themselves in their separate and individual capacities.

—Abraham Lincoln

 The concept of subsidiarity entered the European debate with force in 1989 and 1990, during the preliminary stages of the negotiation of the Maastricht Treaty. Misunderstood and interpreted in numerous different ways, it was generally viewed by public opinion as being another example of Community jargon secreted by a technocratic and distant Europe. The word *subsidiarity* provokes annoyance in some listeners, or a smile. Others receive it with a knowing look, expressing profound skepticism.

Yet the idea is simple. Our societies want to provide considerable freedom and autonomy for individuals, but they also want to pursue efficiently the general interest and the common good. This ambition has applied to Western democracies since the time of ancient Greece. But it does, of course, represent a contradiction.

Absolute freedom leads to anarchy. Absolute efficiency leads to totalitarianism. The subsidiarity concept provides a means to resolve that contradiction. It implies that the collective authority can only intervene where individuals alone are not capable of attaining a recognized and accepted objective, but that in such a case, it must intervene; further, if several levels of authority exist, the collective authority should intervene at the lowest level compatible with the objective pursued: at the level of the village or town rather than at the county level or provincial level; at the provincial level rather than at the national level; and at the European (namely, continental) level where the states are powerless. This approach limits not only the *extent* of collective intervention but also its *distance* in relation to the citizen for whom it is exercised. In principle, it provides individuals with the greatest degree of freedom that is compatible with the general interest. Thus described, this approach is as much a matter of common sense as one of political philosophy, and it ought not to be difficult for public opinion to grasp.

Subsidiarity is profoundly rooted in political thinking in the Western world. Its trace can be found in Aristotle, who describes a society in which family, village, and city each serve a part of the needs of citizens. Saint Thomas considered that since man has an individual relationship with God, he cannot be entirely subordinated to the political community. The role of the latter must be confined to "supplementing, where something is missing; perfecting, if something better can be achieved." The concept was further developed during the Reformation by Althusius, a German jurist, who was Calvinist and influenced by the dominant trends of thought in the Netherlands. He viewed society as a superposition of autonomous communities (family, college, town, province, state) that cannot be assimilated and do not interfere in each other's fields of competence. Some of his ideas are echoed in the United States' Declaration of Independence.

More recently, the subsidiarity principle reappeared in the social doctrine of the Catholic Church from Léon XIII to John-Paul II, from *Rerum novarum* to *Pacem in terris*. "To withdraw from groupings of a lower order, in favour of a larger collective of a higher order, those functions which the former are able to exercise themselves, would not only be to commit an injustice, but would also be to disturb the social order in a very damaging way" (*Quadragesimo Anno* 1931).

Subsidiarity provides a matrix for the sharing of power between different levels of authority; it therefore finds a natural point of application in countries that have a federal structure, such as Switzerland or the United States. "Everyone knows that sovereignty is divided in Switzerland," observes Alexis de Tocqueville. As for the United States: "The idea was to divide sovereignty in such a way that the various states forming the Union would continue to govern themselves in all matters concerning their internal prosperity alone, without preventing the nation from being a single body and providing for all its general needs." Tocqueville concludes thus: "The issue was complex and difficult to resolve." That remains the case today.

Germany is a federal state. It is therefore not surprising that its constitution contains the subsidiarity principle. Article 72, paragraph 2, of the Grundgesetz gives an exhaustive description of the conditions to be satisfied in order for the Bund to be entitled to legislate: efficiency, scope of the consequences, general interest. Until the Maastricht Treaty, that article was the substantive law provision most often cited as an example of the application of the subsidiarity principle.

The connection between subsidiarity and federalism prompted Delors to say that "subsidiarity is, in fact, a form of education in the federal approach." That connection also accounts for the fact that Germany and Belgium, both of which are federal states, were amongst the strongest supporters of the principle during the negotiation of Maastricht.

The subsidiarity principle is almost automatically linked to the exercise of power at different decisionmaking levels. For that reason, it has implicitly been central to the operation of the European institutions since their creation. "In fact, the European nations are creating a supra-national power solely for the purpose of dealing with problems that they can not resolve separately" (Millon-Delsol

1993). The areas of competence transferred to the common institutions are substantial, but the exercise of that competence is limited. Article 5 of the first European treaty, which established the Coal and Steel Community, provided that "the Community shall exert direct influence upon production or upon the market only when circumstances so require." In favoring *directives,* which leave the national authorities free to determine the conditions of application, over *regulations,* which are directly applicable within the member states, the Treaty of Rome (Article 189, now Article 249, of the EC treaty) likewise reveals a spirit of subsidiarity.

However, it was somewhat belatedly that the principle was finally mentioned expressly in European legislation, and this was as a result of the efforts of two men whose convictions are well known: Altiero Spinelli and Jacques Delors.

It appears to have been Spinelli who secured the inclusion of the following passage in the report on the European Union that was being prepared for Léo Tindemans in 1975 by the Commission, of which Spinelli was then a member: "In accordance with the principle of subsidiarity, the Union will be given responsibility only for those matters which the member states are no longer capable of dealing with efficiently." In 1984, it was Spinelli again who, as a member of the European Parliament, ensured that the Parliament adopted a draft treaty on the European Union, Article 12 of which, for the first time in the European context, provided a definition of the subsidiarity principle: "The Union shall only act to carry out those tasks which may be undertaken more effectively in common than by the Member States acting separately, in particular those whose execution requires action by the Union because their dimension or effects extend beyond national borders."

Jacques Delors developed that theme repeatedly during the period leading up to the negotiation of the Maastricht Treaty: in Bonn, before the representatives of the Länder (May 1988); in Strasbourg, before the European Parliament (January 1989); and at the College of Europe in Bruges (October 1989).

Taken up by the European Parliament (on the basis of a report by Giscard d'Estaing) by several member states, including Germany and

Belgium, and for different reasons by the United Kingdom, subsidiarity held an important place in the negotiation of Maastricht. The result is Article 3b (now Article 5 of the EC treaty), which states that the Community shall intervene "only if and in so far as the objectives of the proposed action cannot sufficiently be achieved by the Member States and can therefore, by reason of the scale or effects of the proposed action, be better achieved by the Community."

That article, which is really quite modest, was an object of renewed attention when the Community was seeking to resolve the problem posed by the first Danish referendum, which rejected the Treaty of Maastricht. The European Council, which met in Edinburgh in 1992, devoted an entire section of its conclusions to the interpretation and implementation of Article 3b. Those conclusions were more political than legal, and they were invoked again in the 1996 and 1997 negotiations with a view to adapting them and attaching them to the Treaty of Amsterdam in the form of a protocol. They are not disputed in principle.

However, behind the member states' apparent consensus on subsidiarity as a remedy to genuine or supposed European ills lurk real difficulties on both the theoretical and practical levels. One clearly senses that in the light of experience, several states were reluctant to reopen the debate during the negotiation of the Treaty of Amsterdam. The truth is that the application of the subsidiarity principle is neither simple to conceive nor easy to implement. The concept is ambiguous and the approach often equivocal.

On the theoretical level, the main difficulty stems from the positive or negative slant that can be given to the expression of the principle. Some consider the principle as confining the action of the Union to that which is strictly necessary: a duty of *noninterference*. Others view it as obliging the Union to act where the member states fail: a duty of *intervention*. Those are two sides of the same coin, but the political philosophy differs considerably according to which side is emphasized. Jean-Pierre Cot, a French member of the European

45

Parliament, was once prompted to say: "It is convenient for Mr. Delors to be in agreement with Mrs. Thatcher over a misunderstanding."

Both aspects are present in the wording adopted in the Maastricht Treaty. Article 3b of the treaty implies that the Community should only intervene if the objectives of the envisaged action cannot be achieved sufficiently by the member states, but that the Community shall take action in that case. That ambiguity in the scope of the principle accounts for much of its success.

A second theoretical difficulty stems from the fact that the subsidiarity principle is a political concept based on subjective assessment. That emerges plainly from the successive forms in which the principle has been expressed. In all cases, it is necessary, in the first instance, to determine what cannot be sufficiently achieved by the lower order of power (or what the latter "cannot so well do," in the words of Lincoln), or what can be "better achieved" (or achieved "more efficiently" in the draft treaty presented by Spinelli) at a higher level. That sufficiency or efficiency criterion is obviously subjective, and its assessment is political rather than legal. By introducing this type of consideration into the treaty, its interpretation was left to the Court. In this domain, the Court remains cautious, but it has nevertheless acquired from the Maastricht Treaty a power to assess the relative efficiency of actions performed at the national and Community level. Was that really the considered intention of all member states?

Finally, there is an element of time. The concept of what would be better achieved at the Community level or what is insufficient at the national level will of course vary with time. To the extent that the environment was dealt with during the 1950s, there was no doubt that this was a matter of national or even local competence. Who would deny that there is now a transnational dimension that must be dealt with by the Community? Likewise, in the early days, it was not considered necessary that Europe should involve itself in the fight against terrorism or drugs: it was prompted to do so by the growth of international criminal networks.

These theoretical difficulties explain not only the length and intensity of the debates during the intergovernmental conference leading up to Maastricht, but also the problems raised by the application of the subsidiarity principle within the institutional framework of the Union. One can see why several member states were reluctant to reopen that debate, preferring to retain the existing texts as far as possible.

D ifficulties arise not only on the conceptual level. The implementation of the subsidiarity principle in the daily practice of the Union can prove problematic, as may be illustrated by the examples of headlights, cheese, and beaches.

Headlights. In order to stigmatize abuse of power by the Commission and to denounce the excesses of the Brussels technocracy's urge to harmonize, many French people point to the demise of yellow headlights on motor vehicles. That the color of headlights can give rise to an identity reflex no doubt reflects the importance that cars have assumed as cultural assets. Does subsidiarity not imply that car manufacturers should be free to equip their vehicles with headlamps of any color, provided they serve their lighting purpose?

In fact, the Community provision making white headlights compulsory for vehicles first registered after 1 January 1993 was adopted at the request of the French car manufacturers, who were complaining of the competitive disadvantage they suffered as a result of having to produce one series of cars with yellow headlights (for the French market) and another series with white headlights (for other markets). That provision (Council Directive 91/663 of 10 December 1991) was adopted unanimously by the Council, and hence with France's vote. One can hardly blame the Community technocracy for that.

Cheese. The case of the directive on hygiene for dairy products (Council Directive 92/46 of 16 June 1992) is even more exemplary, for it attracted the attention of the Prince of Wales. At a public gathering in Normandy, the heir to the British throne denounced the Community plot that would lead to the disappearance of a major cultural asset, namely the 250 varieties of cheese of which the French nation is rightly proud. Given the importance of cheese in the daily life of the French, and that the issue arose just as the debate on the ratification of Maastricht was taking place, it is hardly surprising that this opportunity to attack the technocrats was not missed.

In fact, the French know (or ought to know) that most of their cheeses are made from untreated milk. The high level of bacterial activity resulting from that production method is what gives the cheeses their distinctive taste. That is what makes a Camembert develop in smell, taste, and texture as the hours and days go by. However, that proliferation of bacteria raised a problem in connection with the hygiene regulations of certain countries. Furthermore, it is possible, using pasteurized milk, to manufacture cheeses that have the same initial appearance and more or less the same taste as the raw milk cheeses; indeed, that is one of the specialties of the producers of Northern Europe. In this case, with reduced or nonexistent bacterial activity, the cheeses keep well and comply with the strictest regulations. Of course, gourmets consider that alternative to be heretical, or even horrific; but from the point of view of a supermarket manager, a cheese that is presentable in appearance and able to remain on the shelves for several days or weeks without decomposing presents an obvious commercial advantage.

Faced with that commercial threat, the French cheese lobby mobilized to obtain European recognition of labels of origin and acceptance of bacterial levels for raw milk cheeses that are between ten and one hundred times higher than those tolerated for pasteurized milk cheeses. That answered the concerns of the gourmets and satisfied the interests of the main French producers. The protected markets of Northern Europe were to open up. Was it necessary to invoke subsidiarity to prevent that beneficial step? Whatever the Prince of Wales may have thought, the objective and the result of the Community directive were to maintain and protect the diversity of cheeses, and particularly that of French cheeses. That is why France voted in favor of the directive.

Beaches. Why on earth should the Community concern itself with the quality of water on beaches (Council Directive 76/160)? Is that not an obvious example of a breach of the subsidiarity principle?

And yet . . . bearing in mind the annual tourist migrations, millions of Europeans are concerned about the cleanliness of their neighbors' beaches. That is a legitimate concern, for it affects their health and that of their children. How could it be addressed?

The one point on which they agree in this domain is that the assurances given by local authorities are unreliable. No authority of a seaside resort would dare to cast doubt on the cleanliness of its beaches. Stronger guarantees may be given at a regional or national level. However, the French hotel trade has everything to gain from a well-timed disclosure of information concerning the quantities of fecal matter in the waters of the Costa del Sol or the risks of salmonella poisoning on Italian beaches. Whom should one believe? Such reasoning is of course cynical, but is the public not somewhat cynical in this domain?

Hence the idea of entrusting the task of granting the quality label (*the blue flag*) to an authority as distant as possible from local interests and that, having no beaches of its own, is less likely to be influenced by individual interests. That demand from citizens has been relayed by the demands of those resorts that have taken the necessary and often expensive steps to obtain clean waters. In spite of all their precautions, a malicious article or broadcast could ruin a holiday season if there were no authorized reply. The Community label provides that reply. Since the guarantee cannot be issued "in a satisfactory manner" at the lower level, surely the Community is under an obligation to intervene by responding to a demand from the citizens, relayed by substantial and legitimate economic interests.

The directive on bathing water was adopted unanimously.

L et us leave aside the farcical inventions of the British tabloid press, which regularly refers to nonexistent directives concerning the size and shape of cucumbers and bananas. The three cases presented above are among those that are most often cited as examples of abusive Community intervention. They also illustrate that the institutions often face difficult arbitrations.

The subsidiarity principle (in the sense of noninterference) must of course be taken into account, but so, too, must major economic interests that may be implicated, and likewise the legitimate expectations of businesses and citizens vis-à-vis the European institutions, as guardians of the proper functioning of the internal market.

It would be absurd to claim that the arbitration has been perfect in every case. What public authority, in Europe or elsewhere, could fully satisfy that criterion? It is therefore legitimate to examine future legislation, and to re-examine existing legislation, in the light of the subsidiarity principle, without forgetting, however, that it operates in two directions: in the direction of noninterference but also in the direction of intervention. And above all, without forgetting that it is not easy to apply, that it is subjective, changing, and rarely conducive to clear-cut solutions. In short, it is one principle among others that can enlighten the wisdom of the legislator, and it is doubtless important in a structure that is partly federal in its inspiration.

Chapter 6

DEMOCRACY AND COMMUNICATION

A man who has the knowledge but lacks the power to make himself understood is no better off than if he never had any ideas at all.
—Pericles

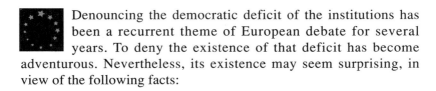 Denouncing the democratic deficit of the institutions has been a recurrent theme of European debate for several years. To deny the existence of that deficit has become adventurous. Nevertheless, its existence may seem surprising, in view of the following facts:

• The European Community is the only international organization ever to have had, within its own structures, an assembly elected directly by the citizens. There has been no other case of this in the world at any time in history. That is certainly one of the distinguishing features of the Community, which makes it difficult to put it in the same category as other international institutions.
• The sphere of competence of the European Parliament, which was initially very limited, has expanded considerably over the years.

The institutional balance has been altered in favor of the Parliament, which, of course, is eminently democratic. In that respect, the Maastricht Treaty introduced significant changes. The co-decision procedure (Article 251 of the EC treaty, Ex-article 189b) gives it a legislative power on a limited number of subjects. The vote of approval (Article 214, paragraph 2, of the EC treaty, Ex-article 158, paragraph 2) regarding the Commission represents the first sketch of a vote of investiture. The Treaty of Amsterdam has extended co-decision and reinforced the approval procedures. In 1999, we saw that the Parliament can compel the Commission to resign.

• However, most of the decisionmaking power within the Community, and even more so within the Union, remains in the hands of the Council. The Council consists of representatives of the governments of the member states, who are democratically answerable to elected assemblies. Its power is evident in the legislative field. As far as the power of execution is concerned, it is either exercised by the member states (as in the case of directives) or delegated to the Commission. But in the latter case, the Commission's action is surrounded by experts whose avowed aim is precisely to ensure, by the obscure workings of commitology, that the views of national governments are heard or, if necessary, that they prevail.

Thus, the democratic principle is very much present, directly or indirectly, within the institutional structure of the European Union. However, that structure itself is heterogeneous and scarcely transparent; it is inspired by both a Community tradition and an intergovernmental tradition, and it consists of pillars and subsystems integrated into a complex and multiform network. Quite naturally, democratic legitimacy within that network takes forms that are as heterogeneous as the structure itself. It is partly based on the European Parliament's own legitimacy, on the role that it plays in the legislative and budgetary spheres, and on the political control that it exercises over the Council and the Commission through the traditional channels of debate, questions, and inquiry commissions. It is also partly based on the legitimacy of each of the national parliaments and on the control that they exercise, or ought to exercise, over government decisions in the various areas of the European decisionmaking process. That dual legitimacy is not perceived by everyone in the same way.

F rom the point of view of the democratic ideal shared by all of the member states, these various forms of parliamentary control ought to be considered as being complementary: a practical and original way of providing democratic legitimacy for a heterogeneous and equally original grouping. In practice, they are usually perceived as being antagonistic. They embrace two distinct theoretical approaches to European integration. Those who take a supranational and Community-orientated view of European integration give precedence to the role of the European Parliament. Those who view it more as an intergovernmental structure give precedence to the role of the national parliaments. In fact, behind the accusations of a democratic deficit leveled at the European institutions, we find the classic debate between integration and cooperation that has marked each stage of the enterprise. The issue is not democracy but the way in which one envisages European union.

In that debate, which easily turns to controversy, some commentators are eager to denounce a lack of democratic legitimacy in the European Parliament. They claim that it is too distant to represent the electorate validly and that the European elections do not attract enough voters to be genuinely representative.

The first argument, concerning distance, can hardly be taken seriously. Can one really suggest that the Luxembourg Parliament, being closer to the citizens it represents, is somehow more legitimate than the Bundestag, the Cortes, or the Commons? If the proximity argument were applied to the internal politics of states, town councils would be considered more legitimate than national parliaments. This argument certainly would be difficult to defend.

The second argument, concerning participation in elections, is likewise unconvincing. In the United States, almost one-third of eligible voters do not bother to register their names on the electoral rolls. Of those who are registered, one quarter generally does not vote. Nevertheless, the president of the United States is validly elected by the majority of those who vote, and no question arises as to the legitimacy of his appointment. In November 1996, President Clinton was re-elected by 24 percent of the registered voters. Who disputes the legitimacy of Clinton? In Britain, because of the way in which the electoral system operates, a government can hold a parliamentary majority on the basis of the votes of a minority of the electorate. Who disputes the legitimacy of the British government? Yet the strongest criticism of the legitimacy of the European Parliament emanates from the United Kingdom.

In a democratic system, beyond arguments of circumstance, any elected assembly enjoys its own legitimacy at each level. It is in nobody's interest to seek to take that legitimacy from it.

There is, however, a political fact that cannot be ignored. Although the democratic principle is present in the European structure, no doubt to the same extent as in many national systems and certainly to a greater extent than in other international organizations, that principle is not perceived as an essential component of the structure but rather as a superficial gloss. The institutions of the Community and of the Union, the *legality* of which is not disputed, lack democratic *legitimacy* in the eyes of public opinion. That divorce between legality and legitimacy warrants further analysis.

One should never underestimate the weight of history and habit in our ancient countries. In countries that have a constitution, the document generally states that "all powers emanate from the nation." However, they emanate in fairly different ways, according to which state is considered. Those differences are the fruits of a past, with its share of heritage and myth. National institutions derive from that past a profound and established legitimacy that is usually uncontested. For the European institutions, the situation is entirely different. Their legitimacy is almost confused with efficiency. It is based on results. Those results are hardly negligible regarding peace, prosperity, security, and involvement in planetary decisions. But the results need only dwindle in one sector or another for the legitimacy of the entire venture to be brought into question. Public opinion is not mobilized by a machine. "One does not fall in love with a big market," said Delors. "What is missing are reasons to get involved, values, or in other words, an ideology and an imaginary" (Wolton 1993).

Strangely enough, at a time when globalization and information technology are rocking the world, the weight of the past can become a factor of stability, of acceptability, and hence of success. "The character of civil society and its intermediate associations rooted as it is in non-rational factors like culture, religion, tradition and other pre-modern sources, will be the key to the success of modern societies in a global economy" (Fukuyama 1995).

It will certainly take time for the European institutions to attain the same degree of legitimacy as the national institutions in the hearts of citizens. But it is equally important to place the facts in their historical context; to view the mass of information as a whole; to convey the extent to which the European structure has erected new political forms on an ancient substratum; to demonstrate how it has provided original solutions to some of the most fundamental problems of our societies while recognizing their diversity; and to remember that the legitimacy of national institutions was not acquired from the outset. "The truth is that the States were constructed little by little, or in fits and starts, in a contingent manner, *before* they gained the (more or less enthusiastic) support of their nationals" (Sellier 1996).

That sense of history, of both past and future, was very much present in the minds of the "founding fathers." It has gradually been erased beneath the weight of routine and technicality. Besides, nobody made much effort to preserve it. Europe was not born at Maastricht, but many are they who did not discover it until that treaty.

Europe is scarcely present in education, despite the fact that education is preparing the future. The European Round Table of Industrialists, which brings together eminent company chairmen from almost all countries of the Union, deplores that situation. It has asked that a European dimension be introduced at all levels of education, so that students may learn to communicate through cultural barriers and work amid this diversity, which is Europe's principal asset. This has yet to be achieved.

To remedy that situation, we need more clarity and transparency, more motivation and talent in communicating, explaining, and presenting. The political thinking of citizens must become accustomed to a change in scale, by shifting from the national level to the European level. In time, the weight of facts, the experience of daily reality, and the size of the problems would no doubt spontaneously produce that result, just as political thinking has moved, in the space of a few centuries, from town or local level to national level, from Machiavelli to Tocqueville. But it is highly unlikely that we can safely wait for that slow and spontaneous change of mentality to come about. The world is developing at an increasing pace. We must also accelerate our recognition of what is at stake. That is a great challenge, one of the greatest of the moment; but only by taking up that challenge will the European institutions be able to gain the moral influence that national institutions derive from history and from long-standing habit. "By moral influence, I mean that which makes a people stand in harmony with its leaders" (Sung 1972).

Nothing has been left unwritten about the lack of transparency in European affairs and the semi-clandestine nature of the negotiations that led to Maastricht and then to Amsterdam! Yet Brussels, where the negotiations take place, has one of the most extensive and sophisticated corps of journalists on the planet, and their role should not be underestimated. They can be seen on the fringe of every meeting, in the corridors of the institutions, and at the countless press conferences that punctuate Community life. There are also the numerous lobbyists and the representatives of nonmember states, professional bodies, or interest groupings, whose principal objective is to perceive and possibly influence what might happen in a meeting before it has even been held.

The truth is that virtually everything is known. Interesting documents remain confidential for only a matter of hours; even those that interest nobody rapidly become known. After a discussion has taken place, it is not very difficult to establish how it progressed and what attitude was adopted by those involved. The individual positions of Commission members, which ought to remain secret to preserve the collegial nature of the institution, frequently appear in the press. One can hardly hope to maintain secrecy when working in eleven different languages, with all the associated translators, interpreters, and secretaries handling fax machines and photocopiers.

Nevertheless, the Community's administrative body has long maintained the principle of confidentiality in its work—a legacy of the national administrations of the founder states. Documents were known in substance, but they were not public. The secrecy of meetings was illusory, but they were not open meetings. It was mainly the influence of the Scandinavian countries, which have a particularly open administrative policy, that caused the situation to change. Today most documents are published, and those that are not are almost invariably available on request. A few of the Council sessions are open, and it is likely that this practice will soon become the rule as far as the Council's legislative function is concerned.

That development is undoubtedly commendable. But does it not circumvent the real problems? The main interest of European citizens is not to have access to European Union documents. Each year, the Council's secretariat distributes 1.5 million pages in each of the eleven languages of the Community. That is indigestible! Their main interest is not to read thousands of pages but to understand what is happening so as to form an opinion. "The central problem of democracy is that news travels faster than opinion" (Wolton 1993).

From that point of view, various obstacles exist. There has, of course, been a certain opacity in the functioning of the system, and that is what Europe is now seeking to remedy. There is opacity in the structures: Who does what? Who is responsible for a decision? Finally, there is a serious opacity regarding objectives: Why is all that being done? What goal is being pursued?

The lack of transparency in the structures is partly due to their originality. The distribution of powers at the European level is different from the traditional model. The fundamental debate revolves around abstract terms: sovereignty, integration, supranationality, subsidiarity, cohesion. It cannot be reduced to the usual categories of national political debate: left and right, rich and poor, intellectuals and manual workers, young and old, capital and province, conservative and progressive, which provide a political philosophy for the vast majority. Then there is language and distance—Brussels is distant and foreign! There are not enough relays between the citizen and European political debate; on a national level, that role is played by the parties, associations. and unions. The European personalities who gathered as the "Club de Florence" around Max Kohnstamm, a former close collaborator of Monnet, to reflect on the future of Europe, noted with regard to the negotiation of Maastricht that "the difficulty stemmed not so much from the (very relative) confidentiality of the negotiations as from the absence of relays which might have rendered the various opinions under consideration intelligible to the public."

That amounts to the fact that there is not, or at least not yet, a European public space, within the meaning that sociologists give to that concept: "a symbolic space in which the discussions or debates pursued by the various political, social, religious, cultural and intellectual figures forming a society clash with and reply to one another" (Wolton 1993). Without a public place, without the Greek agora or the Roman forum, there is no debate and hence no genuine democracy.

As for the lack of agreement over objectives, that is a different problem, and one of the most difficult ones, which is discussed elsewhere.

I t was of course in response to that weakness that the practice of direct democracy was introduced and subsequently developed in European affairs. That practice in itself is no more democratic than the parliamentary regime. Countries that do not resort to referendums are no less democratic as a result. Others, such as Switzerland, that use them extensively, are not more democratic on that account. To take just one example, Belgian and French women obtained the right to vote long before Swiss women. Both systems have their advantages and disadvantages.

In the sphere of international politics, the disadvantages have long been considered as being far greater than the advantages. Almost by definition, a treaty takes the form of a compromise, the sometimes fragile balance of which calls for the kind of detailed analysis that a referendum debate cannot provide. At first sight, the precise scope of a legislative text resulting from difficult negotiations is rarely perceptible. That is plainly illustrated by the Maastricht and Amsterdam Treaties. It is perhaps for that reason that the Italian Constitution does not allow referendums on treaties.

Another factor is that international treaties bind the signatory states in the long term; indeed, that is usually their primary objective. It is fairly natural that the average voter should be more concerned with his immediate problems than with the long term; and those who have the greatest interest in the long term, namely the children of today and tomorrow, do not vote. The two most important postwar treaties are undoubtedly the Washington Treaty, which protected Western Europe by establishing the North Atlantic Treaty Organization (NATO) in 1948, and the Treaty of Paris, which by creating the Coal and Steel Community launched the process of European integration in 1950. In the climate of that time, which was still marked by the antagonisms and horrors of the war, it is unlikely that those treaties would have stood the test of a referendum.

Despite those disadvantages, the use of referendums has gradually spread, because they satisfy a demand that has more to do with communication than with democracy. Since there are no relays between the citizen and European debate, it was thought that the citizen should decide on it directly. In one sense, that represents an abdication. It reflects the representation crisis in Western societies, the distance between governors and governed that has emerged clearly over the past few years. On many issues, in almost all countries, the collective opinion of political leaders is not shared by the majority of citizens. The political message is no longer getting through, or has difficulty doing so.

The example that has given greatest cause for consideration, because it arose at a crucial moment, is that of Denmark. On 12 May 1992, the Folketing, which is the Danish parliament, approved the

Treaty of Maastricht by 130 votes against 25, in other words by a majority of five to one. Three weeks later, on 2 June, the referendum produced a majority of 50.7 percent against the treaty, causing consternation throughout the Union. What that vote, like others, brings into question is not only the treaty but also, in Denmark and elsewhere, the confidence of the leaders in the representative democracy on which their legitimacy is based. "The main function of a politician is now professional management of collective perceptions" (Guéhenno 1993). Does that enable one to lead a country?

Though not necessarily convincing from the point of view of democracy, the referendum has demonstrated its efficiency from the point of view of communication. All of the surveys show that knowledge of European affairs is greater in countries that use referendums than in those that do not. It was thanks to the 1992 referendum that the European debate entered French political life with unprecedented intensity. However, it does not resolve the problem of relays; it circumvents it. The European structure will remain fragile if it is merely the preserve of elites incapable of conveying their convictions; if it is not the subject of genuine debate; and if it continues to depend on the episodic and unpredictable voting of national electorates.

Jacques Delors once wondered what the result would have been during the Middle Ages had there been a referendum on the building of cathedrals. The faith of the faithful would no doubt have triumphed, despite the immense cost and endless duration of the works; but that faith itself had been instilled and maintained by clerics, who for generations had relayed the Word. A referendum is merely a moment. It does not allow one to dispense with relays. Where are the clerics now?

Chapter 7

COHESION AND DIVERSITY

Where solidarity is apparent, it is not necessarily natural. It must therefore be organised.

—*Jean Monnet*

The idea of developing and organizing within an institutional framework that which draws the European nations together, their implicit cohesion, so as to overcome the tensions that stem from their diversity, is central to the process of European integration. To substitute a sense of solidarity for the tradition of confrontation is the very essence of the enterprise launched by Schuman and Monnet.

It was the conviction of "a destiny henceforward shared," stated in the Preamble to the Treaty of Paris, that justified the combining of the coal and steel industries. "The designation of a new general interest, extending over several nations, reflects the conviction that there is a common cultural identity which goes deeper than the conflict-fuelling differences" (Millon-Delson 1993). That conviction also accounts for the fact that, contrary to the most firmly rooted diplomatic traditions, small countries are given a weight in the institutional structures that is disproportionate to their size. The idea is not to dominate a disparate grouping but to lead each of the partners, in spite of their diversity, to acknowledge that they share common interests.

That concern for cohesion, solidarity, and interdependency is evident in the gradual implementation of Community policies. In postwar Europe, the idea was to share the management of strategic and scarce resources, namely coal and steel. Later, the European Atomic Energy Community (EURATOM) treaty extended that joint control to nuclear energy, which was viewed as one of the keys to the future that would hopefully be shared. Alain Peyrefitte has pointed out that of the two treaties signed in Rome in March 1957, it was, at the time, EURATOM that seemed most important.

In the burgeoning Community of the 1960s, the implementation of the common agricultural policy expressed solidarity between town and country. It mobilized up to 70 percent of the budgetary resources (less than 50 percent today) and reconciled de Gaulle with the Treaty of Rome. During the 1980s it was the solidarity and interdependency between European regions that was manifest in the spectacular growth of the structural funds. Those funds enabled Ireland, Greece, Spain, and Portugal to become more fully integrated in Community life. From the Single European Act onward, that action was referred to as the "cohesion policy." It was further developed by the Maastricht Treaty, and one-third of the budget is now applied to it. In fact, all of the Community's policies are aimed at increasing its cohesion, either by distributing resources (fishing), pooling means (research), defining common rules (competition), or compensating handicaps (regional policy).

The same applies to external relations. The perception of interdependency, with solidarity as its consequence and cohesion as its objective, is obviously what inspires the first faltering steps of political cooperation. The Davignon report, which marked the starting point of that cooperation in 1970, refers to a "Europe assured of its internal cohesion" and states that it brings together states that, despite their national differences, "are united in their essential interests." That approach explains the constant search for common positions in Middle Eastern affairs, for joint action in the successive stages of the Conference on Security and Cooperation in Europe, and for identical votes at the annual General Assembly of the United Nations.

One example of solidarity, among others, can be found in the support given to the United Kingdom during the Falklands crisis in 1982. No military alliance covered that distant territory, but it seemed natural, independently of the fundamental causes of the conflict, to support a partner whose territory had been invaded.

In the Maastricht Treaty, that same logic is expressed in the arguably excessive or premature ambition for a common external and security policy. The absence of such a policy, in Bosnia, for example, is badly viewed by many Europeans, precisely because it is a demonstration of incoherence.

The common policies that have gradually been implemented, both within and outside the Union, are manifestations of a genuine solidarity, of a desire for cohesive action that distinguishes the Union from free trade areas, where markets are simply opened up on a passive basis.

Yet diversity has also been part of the European integration process from the outset. In the first founding texts, special provisions were already being incorporated for Berlin and East Germany, for overseas territories, and for the Benelux countries. Certain products, such as sugar and bananas, were already the subject of specific agreements departing from common rules.

Successive enlargements have increased that diversity. They entail transition periods—extensive in some cases—during which the new member states are exempted from the treaty rules, to give them time to adapt to those rules (or, conversely, they may be excluded from common policies, where a fear of overly brutal competition arises). Many protocols attached to the treaties determine the case of territories that have a special status, such as Gibraltar, Madeira and the Azores, Mount Athos, the Faroe Islands, Lapland, or the Åland Islands.

The same applies to the new treaties, such as the Single European Act and the Maastricht and Amsterdam Treaties. The numerous declarations and protocols attached to those agreements seek to take specific situations into account. Denmark has become an expert in this domain, especially since the events surrounding the ratification of the Maastricht Treaty. Countless pages of exceptions deal with secondary residences, the environment, monetary union, citizenship, defense, justice, and internal affairs. The true legal scope of those provisions is sometimes dubious, but they do at least bear witness to the will to accommodate difficulties encountered by one partner.

If we add that virtually all of the directives, particularly those concerning the internal market, contain exceptions, transitional provisions, or opt-out clauses, it becomes clear that respect for diversity is solidly anchored in Community life. The image of a standardizing and centralizing Community is purely polemical. It does not stand up to a detailed analysis of European law. In reality, the entire European integration process is marked by a dialectic relationship between the necessary cohesion of the Union and the equally necessary diversity of the parts. Depending on the country, time, and speaker in question, greater emphasis is placed on one necessity than on the other, but any excessive move in either direction prompts a contrary reaction. That, indeed, is why the European venture as a whole now takes the form of a complex network of diversified relations centered on the Community, rather than that of a uniform and monolithic structure.

The cohesion and diversity of the Union are perhaps best illustrated in the monetary domain. That is not a recent phenomenon. Returning from a systematic visit of all member states, Léo Tindemans observed in 1975 that "in the various countries of the Community, those with whom I spoke everywhere recognised the need for a European economic and monetary policy." Further on, he concluded that "progress as regards economic and monetary policy may be sought initially between certain States." Three years later, on the initiative of Valéry Giscard d'Estaing and Helmut Schmidt, that idea was to give birth to the European monetary system.

Monetary union, as conceived in 1988–1989 by the committee

that was then chaired by Delors, and incorporated into the Treaty of Maastricht, is a remarkable cohesion factor. It not only extends but also consolidates the internal market, the survival of which would be constantly brought into question were it to remain exposed to the permanent risk of monetary fluctuations. It is a logical consequence of the free movement of capital, and it requires all actual or potential participants to exercise the same discipline in managing their respective budgets and economies, so as to attain the degree of economic convergence without which there could be no common monetary policy. The "stability pact" initiated by Minister Theo Waigel and adopted in December 1996 by the European Council in Dublin, is simply the legal embodiment of that obligation.

However, the different economic situations of the member states and their unequal ability to assume all of the obligations of monetary union at a specific time led the authors of the Maastricht Treaty to organize the move to a single currency as a stage-by-stage process. The conditions, criteria, and procedures governing that move were the subject of lengthy negotiations. It was not easy to recognize and accept the consequences of the diversity of situations within such a central sector of the Union without compromising its cohesion. The complex institutional solutions that were adopted represent one of the treaty's most original features. The Club de Florence refers to institutional osmosis and notes that "the monetary union provisions of the Maastricht Treaty provide a good example of a balance between the interests of those who are forging ahead and those whose political will or ability to follow them is lacking." However, in the eyes of public opinion, the cohesion objective was far more visible than the idea of allowing for diversity.

When the Maastricht Treaty was signed, the European leaders were unanimous in considering that the monetary provisions were the essential point of the negotiations that had just ended and one of the keys to the future of the European integration process. Delors spoke of a "genuine revolution." Since that time, economic and monetary union and the means to achieve and subsequently maintain it, or for some, the need to exclude it, have been a central concern in all member states. The political debate has focused on that subject to such an extent that some observers have been prompted to speak of a "correct view," implicitly criticizing leaders for excluding any alternative and for allowing themselves to be dominated by a single objective without sufficiently measuring its consequences. It is true to say that the ongoing effort to maintain tight budgetary control with a view to achieving or sustaining monetary union affects all areas of life. It is felt by everyone. Some consider it deplorable, without wondering whether such measures might not have been necessary in any case, after so many years of lax policies. But apart from the United Kingdom and Denmark, which have secured a special status with regard to monetary union, few voices expressed a desire to be part of a second wave. Almost all of the member states wanted to be among the front-runners, even if that required heroic efforts. Is the cohesion argument *that* convincing?

The debate would have been clearer had it been emphasized that monetary union is not, in itself, the final goal. It is one piece of the puzzle; an important and in some respects essential means to achieving a level of solidarity and cohesion enabling European countries to defend their interests more easily in a global economy. It will have a decisive influence on the future of European integration. But it is the European structure itself, the results it has already achieved in terms of peace, tranquillity, prosperity, tolerance, solidarity, and influence, to the great benefit of European citizens, and also the results that it promises to achieve in the future that are fundamental, and not the means to achieve them. That argument is presumably too abstract to have much chance of being heard!

For the citizen, money is a tangible matter. It concerns everyone, because nobody can do without it. To some people, it represents one of the major purposes of existence. That accounts for the unusual fact that a European objective, namely the single currency, was immediately grasped by public opinion, even though it was not universally accepted from the outset. The "Maastricht criteria" have entered into the everyday language of all countries of the Union. Viewed by some as providing the keys to political wisdom, they are positively despised by others. Obviously, they merit neither that excessive reverence nor that excessive disgrace. They are simply a

66

means—imperfect like so many others—to achieve the goal that the signatories of the Maastricht Treaty collectively set themselves.

A nother classic illustration of the dialectic relationship between cohesion and diversity is provided by the countries that would like to become members of the European Union. Here, the discussion takes the form of a debate between enlargement and deepening, between the partisans of an *intensive* Europe, in which cohesion would be optimized, and those of an *extensive* Europe, with increased diversity. That, of course, is a false debate, because within the bounds of the continent, Europe could not renounce enlargement without failing to fulfill its vocation, and neither could it renounce deepening without losing its dynamics. Just as it has always been necessary to reconcile cohesion and diversity, it will also always be necessary to try to reconcile enlargement and deepening.

So far, that has been achieved. The first enlargement, which concerned the United Kingdom, Denmark, and Ireland, was preceded by the setting up of political cooperation through the Davignon report, and by an initial attempt at monetary union, through the Werner report. The entry of Spain and Portugal coincided with the adoption of the Single European Act, which defined the cohesion policy and, by extending majority voting, enabled the internal market to be created. The entry into force of the Maastricht Treaty, which opens the way to monetary union, came shortly before the accession of Sweden, Finland, and Austria. In the European symphony, enlargement and deepening are superposed in counterpoint. The Treaty of Amsterdam ought to have introduced the institutional changes required for further enlargement. Because it did not do so, a further intergovernmental conference looms on the horizon.

It is true that the issue is now particularly sensitive, for several reasons:

- The previous enlargements concerned two or three countries; there are now twelve candidates knocking at the door.
- The institutional model adopted by the six founding member

states has been transposed, without any major modification, to fifteen; it is showing signs of pressure, and the question arises as to whether it could operate with twenty-five or thirty participants.

- The internal debate is bringing out old but fundamental differences of opinion as to the nature and future of the enterprise: under those circumstances, to extend the Union can be a pretext for denaturing it.

Beyond the debate on enlargement, it is of course the very nature of the Union that is at stake. This is the most recent version of a debate that has always existed between the supporters of a free trade area and those who favor a more strongly structured Community. If it were enlarged without precautions, without institutional changes, without defined goals, the Union would rapidly be reduced to a mere common market or free trade area. Some might be satisfied with that, but others are not prepared to see the joint efforts of several decades erased.

To face that challenge, it seemed necessary to move from diversity, which has always existed, toward differentiation, which is a structured and organized form of diversity. The idea was to incorporate into the treaty a legal basis for diversity within the framework of the Union. Those who wanted to forge ahead should be able to use the common institutions and the Community method to fulfill their ambitions without disregarding the *acquis communautaire* that they share with other member states or indeed the interests of the nonparticipants. That is difficult but not impossible to achieve.

In fact, that idea emerged from a variety of sources under different names, before playing a major role in the intergovernmental negotiations in 1997. It was the *hard core* in a document produced by the German Christian Democrat Party in September 1994; at the same time, it was *flexibility* for John Major, *concentric circles* for Edouard Balladur, and the distinction between *Europe-area (Europe-espace)* and *Europe-power (Europe-puissance)* for Giscard d'Estaing. It was *reinforced cooperation* in the letter of President Jacques Chirac and Chancellor Helmut Kohl in December 1995, and *differentiation* in the joint memorandum of the Benelux countries in March 1996. The Club de Florence refers to an implicit pact underpinning the Union: "Whilst no State can be forced to participate against its will in an integration step, it is equally unthinkable that the more reluctant parties should prevent those who wish to forge ahead from doing so." National sovereignty cannot be invoked by a state as a means to constrain other states.

Whether the provisions of the Treaty of Amsterdam in this respect are sufficiently precise and operational to meet the expectations and the target is very much an open question. These provisions will no doubt have to be re-examined during future negotiations.

Chapter 8

POWER AND IMPOTENCE

A vast quivering mass of tormented, hungry, careworn and bewildered human beings gape at the ruins of their cities and homes, and scan the dark horizons for the approach of some new peril, tyranny or terror.

—*Sir Winston Churchill*

 In 1950, the European integration process grew out of a profound sense of impotence. To gauge the extent of that feeling, one really needs to have lived through that period. It was the physical impotence of destroyed towns and factories, of rawboned populations, and difficult communications. It was the psychological powerlessness to cope with the drama of the past, the spite and the hatred of the victorious and the defeated that each side in turn had been. It was also the political impotence, the shameful weakness of disorientated governments hurrying to Washington to collect a few dollars as a viaticum.

At that time, the European countries seemed incapable of controlling their destiny, of organizing the reconstruction of society, of expressing a collective ambition and putting aside what appeared to be the imminent prospect of a further war.

Monnet's memoirs, like Churchill's speeches, admirably

describe that atmosphere of oppressive fear and renewed anxiety. "In the current state of the world, wherever one turns there are only dead-ends to be found," wrote Monnet. At the same time, Spaak referred to "expressions of impotence" in connection with the debates of the Council of Europe. That was the soil in which Schuman's venture sprouted and from which it drew its initial dynamics. "A leap into the unknown," he said on the evening of his speech of 9 May 1950, but the unknown certainly seemed preferable to a repetition of the past.

The idea of overcoming resurgent antagonisms by merging the coal and steel industries, which were factors of power, and by controlling them jointly for the purposes of "a destiny henceforward shared," represented an untrodden path. In a world full of resentment, fear, and skepticism, Europeans were being told that they could one day recover a degree of control over their destiny, provided that they exercised it together. That message marked a generation that placed its faith, its intelligence, but also a great deal of emotion and sometimes passion in the European integration process. The frustrated nationalism that had torn Europe apart and was reappearing everywhere could be sublimated in a shared venture.

Today, when the emotion has subsided, what remains is the Franco-German reconciliation kindled by that venture. Durably consolidated by de Gaulle and Konrad Adenauer in the Elysée Treaty, that reconciliation closed a wound that threatened each generation with a new war. The events in Yugoslavia bear witness to what happens when such wounds remain open. In Western Europe, that progress toward peace is considered irreversible. Nevertheless, it is worth noting that even now, in Ireland, in the Basque territory, in Corsica, and sometimes elsewhere, nationalism fuels young people to such an extent that they are willing to die and to kill. That disease is contagious, and we should heed the danger it presents. "War is not only the past; it can be our future" (Mitterand 1995).

In any event, it is important to grasp that it was by offering *powerless* nations the prospect of exercising together a collective *power* that age-old enmities were overcome, that a common enterprise was launched, and that a lasting peace process was made possible. That dialectic between power and impotence has been central to the European integration process from the outset.

Twenty-five years later, touring the capitals to prepare his report on the European Union, Tindemans caught a similar echo: "During my visits I was struck by the widespread feeling that we are vulnerable and powerless." In 1975, this was no longer the miserable impotence of the postwar years but the impotence of old nations in a postcolonial world that had just experienced an oil crisis. "Our peoples expect the European Union to be, where and when appropriate, the voice of Europe. Our joint action must be the means of effectively defending our legitimate interests; it must provide the basis for real security in a fairer world, and enable us to take part in this dialogue between groups which clearly characterises international life." That is what led Tindemans to make external relations a priority. They became "one of the main reasons for building Europe."

At the time when that report was published, the member states of the Community had already been endeavoring for five years, on a very modest level, to coordinate their respective foreign policies on the basis of the Davignon report. That report had introduced, in the field of foreign policy, procedures for informal consultation, reciprocal information, and deliberation that, if all went well, could culminate in joint declarations or even joint action. Those efforts, which until Maastricht were referred to as "European political cooperation," developed gradually. The obvious aim was to gain a certain collective hold on the international environment of the Community. Europe had to "make its voice heard in world affairs" (Copenhagen report, 1973), and to that end, it was necessary "that Europe should unite and speak with one voice, if it wished to be heard and to play its rightful role" (document on European identity, 1973). "The Ten should seek increasingly to shape events, and not simply to react to them" (London report, 1981). The aim of all that, as stated in the Preamble to the Single European Act in 1986, was to enable Europe "more effectively to protect its common interest and independence," or in other words, to acquire a form of power. This was tentative collective response to the sense of powerlessness described in the Tindemans report.

The political cooperation that existed on the eve of the negotiation of Maastricht was probably the most systematic, far-reaching, and lasting diplomatic coordination that has ever been achieved between sovereign states. Its importance should therefore not be overlooked, but its scope remained limited. It operated aside from the Community structures, without instruments of its own, which often made it seem platonic and declaratory. It shared the weaknesses of all cooperation procedures: in the event of disagreement, even by one single member state, nothing happened. As Tindemans said, "It explicitly incorporates within its structure the possibility of failure: the pursuit of different policies whenever co-ordination has not been achieved." Finally, issues of security and defense were excluded from its scope.

The political cooperation of the 1980s was a useful instrument, well suited to a bipolar and stable world in which all security problems concerning Europe were dealt with by NATO.

However, at the time when the negotiations that led to the Maastricht Treaty began, Germany was reunified, Eastern Europe was swaying uneasily toward democracy and a market economy, and the geopolitical situation of the continent was so radically altered that the security issues were taking on a completely new dimension. Political cooperation, as practiced for the previous twenty years, then seemed ill suited to the challenges of the moment. "Twenty years of foreign policy co-operation have provided better knowledge of one another and a certain harmonisation of diplomatic working methods, sometimes yielding unanimous positions. But that is not enough" (Delors 1991).

I t has often been said and written that the Maastricht Treaty was the last document inspired by the Cold War: a diplomatic dinosaur unsuited to the new environment, a "historic stupidity," and the fruit of the collective political short-sightedness of the European leaders.

European integration, having resulted from the Soviet threat, must obviously disappear with the latter!

In light of the facts, that argument does not stand up. In the fear-ridden twilight of the postwar years, the Soviet threat certainly contributed to the coalescence of Western Europe. "Timor externus maximus concordiae vinculum," said Livy: external threat is the greatest factor of concord. But even in 1975, when Tindemans was analyzing the various motivations behind European integration, it was not the Soviet threat but the decline of Europe's influence on the world stage that was the primary concern. The spectacular progress made by Europe during the 1980s—the Single European Act, the internal market, and the first step toward monetary union—was entirely unconnected with the Soviet threat. The Cold War played no role in it.

The negotiation of Maastricht, confused and complex as it was in its unfolding and in its results, was pursued with two main objects: to obtain monetary cohesion within the Union and to develop a capacity for external action. With the possible exception of the United Kingdom, those two ambitions were shared by all member states. They reflected a desire to adapt European integration to the new geopolitical climate and, in both cases, to increase the power of Europe.

In everyone's interest, a reunited Germany had to be tied into a firmly structured body. "I want a European Germany, not a German Europe," said Kohl and Hans Dietrich Genscher.

It was also necessary to clarify the role that Eastern and Western leaders wanted the Community to play in the consolidation of Central and Eastern Europe. The key date was that of the Group of 7 Summit (meeting of the seven most industrialized nations in the world), held in Paris in 1989, which made the Community responsible for coordinating Western aid for the new democracies on the East side of the continent. This was the first time that the United States, as the Western superpower, relied on Europe to accomplish a strategic task. With its mandate from the West, the Community was perceived in Central and Eastern Europe as a model society, the main source of aid, inspiration, and leadership.

How could the Community be made capable of accomplishing those missions, if not by increasing its collective power? That is exactly what the Maastricht Treaty sought to do, albeit with very variable success. "Europe was not ready to fill the political space that had suddenly been liberated" (Duhamel 1995).

The gradual implementation of economic and monetary union represents the Maastricht Treaty's main contribution to the European integration process. Through the treaty, the single currency—an old ambition long considered illusory—became an accessible goal—difficult, of course, but not out of reach. Since then, despite the difficulties over ratification and despite monetary storms, the political commitment of the main partners, which underlies and justifies the provisions of the treaty, has never failed. In terms of political analysis, that is a remarkable fact, a fundamental choice that will quite obviously have an impact on both the internal and external life of the Union.

The target of a single currency is connected with the internal development of the European Union. The initiative taken by Delors in 1988 at the European Council meeting in Hanover was an extension of the internal market and, in particular, of the free movement of capital. In an open market, speculative movements can put unbearable pressure on exchange rates at any time. That has already been witnessed on several occasions. The resulting devaluations, whether justified or not, consequently bring into question the operation and strength of the internal market. "A single market without a single currency is only half the battle" (European Round Table of Industrialists 1991).

However, that aim also has an external dimension. "If the single currency materialises and enables the Old Continent to become an area of monetary stability with a strong currency, the Union will assume the status of a world monetary power alongside Japan and the United States, and it will be able to work with them towards improved regulation of the international monetary system" (Cohen-Tanugi 1995). Prior to the adoption of a single currency, despite the

European Union's status as the leading commercial power, its weight within the international monetary system did not reflect that situation. In the commercial sphere, it acts jointly, as in the lengthy negotiation of the Uruguay Round. In the monetary sphere, the member states acted separately, which usually meant that they accepted solutions imposed by others. Monetary union remedies that situation, which may account for the fact that it is not universally welcomed. "The single currency is also an instrument of power" (Delors 1994).

F ew things have harmed the image of the European Union in the eyes of public opinion as much as the spectacle of our collective impotence in Bosnia. I refer of course to political impotence; many people are unaware that the Union and its member states, in Bosnia and elsewhere (Rwanda, for example), provided 80 percent of the humanitarian aid to help cope with the consequences of the civil war and of the carnage. Likewise, it is European countries that are welcoming almost 1 million refugees from the former Yugoslavia who are fleeing the barbarity of their neighbors. Germany has taken in more than 300,000 of these refugees, which represents an annual budgetary expense of 4 billion marks. Thus, Europe has not remained inactive, but when it came to imposing peace on the warlords, it was NATO and the United States that played the decisive role. However precarious it may be, the peace was made in Dayton. Europe had little involvement in that process. Or at least, that is how the events have been perceived. In Kosovo, European involvement was greater, but nevertheless the basic conclusion remains similar.

Would things have been entirely different had Europe been unified, strong, and able to project an effective military force? That is not certain. History, and particularly the history of Europe, has shown that strength, money, and good advice from outside do not always suffice to maintain peace and resolve crises. Long periods of suffering, the sacrifice of generations, and many mass graves and ossuaries are sometimes required before good sense ultimately triumphs over the madness and passions of humankind. It also takes enlightened political leaders who know how to appeal to that good sense, and to the morality and spiritual values of nations. The passage of time, which enables one to forget, is often necessary. In other words, many crises cannot be resolved in the short term, which ought to instill a sense of modesty in diplomats and politicians.

In the case of Bosnia, the question did not arise, because Europe was neither unified, nor strong, nor determined. However, it is important to note that public opinion would have liked things to be different. Those who criticize the impotence of Europe are implicitly saying that they wish Europe had been able, or that it might one day be able, to exercise an external force, the absence of which they deplore. That sentiment is not new. It obviously inspired the proposal made by Mitterand and Kohl in April 1990, to negotiate the implementation of a common foreign policy. Of all the objectives of Maastricht, that was certainly the one that found most sympathy in public opinion.

Despite that support, one can hardly say that the result met the expectations. The Maastricht Treaty fixed the objective without providing any of the instruments required to attain it. There was no provision for common reflection and analysis, nor a political motor to initiate action, nor any operational decisionmaking procedure, nor any visible and collective enforcement instrument. Those omissions did not occur by chance or through the incompetence of the negotiators. They reflect the clear intention of the member states, or at least that of the principal member states, to avoid surrendering any of the instruments of power in this domain. Inspired by the logic of European integration and by the scale of the challenges to be faced, the member states wish, in principle, to engage in joint action. Held back by the spontaneous conservatism of their authorities and by the natural desire of political figures to keep, at least in appearance, for themselves alone the decisionmaking power, those same states are unwilling to give up anything in favor of that shared ambition. The paradox lies in the gap between the declared objective and the available instruments; and from that paradox stems impotence.

Those considerations were very much in the minds of the negotiators during the intergovernmental conference of 1996. They had been instructed to review the provisions adopted at Maastricht, and particularly those concerning foreign and security policy. The lessons that everyone could draw from the failure of Maastricht in this respect seemed obvious:

- To obtain results, it is not sufficient to express ambitions.
- One must first acquire the instruments required to fulfill them.
- Above all, for an instrument to be useful, there must be a will to use it.

The last point is undoubtedly the most essential of the three. Stuart Eizenstat, a perceptive and benevolent observer and former U.S. ambassador to the European Union, who is now undersecretary of state in Washington, describes it in these terms:

> Key members do not yet wish to relinquish their foreign policy prerogatives in favour of a common approach. I believe that until this change has occurred the common policy will always be less than the Maastricht Treaty promised. . . . The European Union will not develop the political and diplomatic muscle compatible with its economic and trade clout until the key members desire it, which at this point they do not.

The Treaty of Amsterdam certainly improves the instrument: the means for analysis, forecasting, proposals, financing, and external representation are provided for. What will also be required is a strong political will, projected by the new "High Representative for External Policy and Security" and supported by public opinion, to bring the national diplomatic services to make full use of that new instrument, enabling it gradually to establish its influence and capacity for action. That process will not be automatic. "The Maastricht revision process should therefore be designed as much as a public debate on the external reach of the Union as a negotiation among governments," said Reinhardt Rummel of the Wissenschaft und Politik Institute in Ebenhausen, before the negotiations had even begun. He added that "the chance for a wider political debate on a major part of the political union should not be missed." In fact, that debate has never really taken place. As a result, the outlook remains uncertain.

E ven greater uncertainty appears when one steps from the diplomatic domain into the military. Nicole Gnesotto, director of the WEU Institut for Security Studies in Paris, who has examined these problems extensively, concludes regretfully that "for forty years, defence was one of the most elusive sea-snakes of the European integration process, and its failure is fundamentally intertwined with the failure of political Europe." What causes this failure?

During the postwar years, Europe learned to live in a bipolar world. Under the Soviet threat, the continent was defended, to everyone's satisfaction, by a trans-Atlantic alliance. Within that alliance, the weight of the United States and of its nuclear arsenal was the decisive factor. After the failure of the European Defense Community proposal in 1955, the idea of a genuinely European defense structure remained purely speculative and was formally excluded by the dominant orthodoxy that placed an exclusive emphasis on NATO and its integrated commands. "To avoid European integration, Atlantic integration was increased" (Froment-Meurice 1984). The prospect of a European defense structure seemed all the more unrealistic and inappropriate because since 1966 France had withdrawn from NATO. In fact, the strategic options of the European countries were probably less disparate than they seemed. But in appearance, they were disparate, and without a visibly shared strategic option, no common defense could be envisaged.

The fall of the Berlin Wall, the implosion of the Soviet Union, and the disappearance of any external threat fundamentally altered the strategic situation. That is what led the Maastricht negotiators to consider, for the first time since the failure of the European Defense Community in 1955, the prospect of a common defense in a European framework. That constituted a major innovation, and it is in that context that the revitalization of the Western European Union, the transfer of its headquarters to Brussels, and the creation of the

Eurocorps should be viewed. NATO's recognition of the legitimacy of a European defense identity (Berlin, June 1996) confirmed that course.

However, the debates that were pursued during the intergovernmental conferences in 1996 and 1997 indicated that as far as the main actors are concerned, NATO remains the privileged, if not exclusive framework within which to debate security issues. Closer links between France and the conventional NATO structure, which have yet to be finalized, have enabled an informal group of major countries to operate alongside the United States, determining the main policies and making strategic decisions.

The future will determine whether this form of directorate, referred to as a "caucus" in NATO jargon, is capable of operating effectively on a lasting basis. Previous attempts, particularly during the postwar years, were weakened quite quickly by differences of opinion, which led to internal dissent and ultimately to public disagreement. But in the short term, discrete intergovernmental procedures and the very nature of the alliance combine apparent efficiency with a reduced political cost.

By concerted efforts within that specific framework, major European countries aim to recover at least some of the power that they are no longer able to exercise alone; and because the arrangement is informal and discrete, they succeed in doing so without the further and, above all, visible concessions of national sovereignty that they would have to make if a European defense structure were set up in the context of the Union. Obviously, some concessions to the U.S. leadership are required, but they are less visible, and public opinion has gradually become accustomed to them over the years.

That approach also offers several benefits to the other, smaller countries that do not belong to the "caucus." The pacifist, neutralist reflexes that are evident in their political life and that have been increased by the removal of any sense of threat need not be confronted. Those reflexes stem from geography, history, moral convictions, or rejection of all that was unbearable and odious in the European wars or in certain colonial enterprises. The projection of force, as an instrument of external policy, is repugnant to many European citizens, particularly in countries that historically have suffered from it. Even those who would like the Union to play a strong and active role in international life do not accept all of the consequences of that role, in particular the budgetary consequences.

Any form of power will seem abusive and corrupt to some observers, particularly where it is exercised over others. But although the superior forms of generosity come from the heart and not from the wallet, there are less noble forms that can be exercised only by being rich, or in other words, powerful. Although not every form of peace must be maintained by force, some forms depend on it. The *pax Christi* that practicing Christians wish each other on Sundays comes from the heart and soul; but the *pax romana* was based on the legions.

Ten years ago, certain voices in the United States were calling for a military and political retreat from the European continent. That caused a degree of concern in Europe. Nowadays, Washington seems more intent on maintaining a long-term political and military presence on the European continent. Richard Holbrooke, the deputy secretary of state in 1995, expressed that intention as follows: "The United States has become a European power in a sense that goes beyond traditional assertions of America's commitment to Europe. In the twenty-first century, Europe will still need the active American involvement that has been a necessary component of the continental balance for half a century." Because the United States considers itself a European power and part of the continental balance, it does not want there to be any debate, let alone any decision in its absence on essential issues of European security and defense. That is understandable. In this context, the European defense identity should develop exclusively within the framework of NATO.

How, then, should one interpret the ambition to implement, within the Union, a European defense policy leading to a common defense? It would certainly be difficult, though not impossible, to reconcile that aim, expressed in the Treaty of Maastricht and reiterated in the Treaty of Amsterdam, with the trans-Atlantic relationship. But, for a start, the matter would have to be debated. Yet, on the east side of the Atlantic, where a debate exists, in the United Kingdom and elsewhere, on European developments, there was until very recently little or no debate on security and defense.

It is not impossible, and it is even likely, that for reasons of convenience or tradition, because the threat is nonexistent or at least distant and because the American big brother is still present, Europe may once again abstain from clarifying the uncertainties and contradictions that have long permeated any discussion on defense issues in the European context. For that to change, there would have to be a strong impetus and a thorough debate. The first signs of that debate can perhaps be seen in the conclusions of the Anglo-French summit held at Saint-Malo in December 1998, which seemed to suggest that there was a will to further the development of a common defense policy. That would be in keeping with the logic of European integration, which has sought from the outset to enable member states to exercise a collective power together. "European Union will not be complete until it has drawn up a common defence policy," observed Tindemans in 1975. Manfred Wörner, who as secretary-general of NATO ought not to be suspected of being a Euro-centrist, declared fifteen years later: "The European Union without a defence identity would be incomplete and would condemn Europe to playing an essentially rhetorical role in world affairs."

B ut nations, like individuals, often have contradictory ambitions. The members of the European Union wanted and still want to participate in the most ambitious joint venture of the century; however, to an even greater extent in military matters than in diplomacy, they seem unwilling to relinquish any of the means required to fulfill that ambition.

In a world in which the sovereignty of states is being eroded by their interdependency, power is no longer defined mainly in terms of control and domination but in terms of influence and access to the planetary decisionmaking level. The European Union offers its member states access to that decisionmmaking level. It has already acquired that access in the economic and commercial fields. In the Treaty of Maastricht, it expressed a wish to extend it to the monetary, diplomatic, and security fields. That wish is confirmed in the Treaty of Amsterdam. Like any collective ambition, its realization depends on the existence of a firm determination to share the means to fulfill it. That determination is far more important than the provisions of the treaty. Power sharing is the price to be paid to overcome the relative weakness of the participants. Does that determination really exist?

The conviction of the main European governments involved appears today to be strong with regard to currency, but unequal and uncertain elsewhere. It may then be necessary to prolong yet further the bitter experience of impotence.

Chapter 9

COMPETITION AND SOLIDARITY

Some people espouse the first item of information that they encounter with such folly that all other items are merely concubines to them.

—*Baltasar Gracian*

 Paul Krugman, a professor of economics at the Massachusetts Institute of Technology, has explained the cyclic nature of successive bodies of consensus on economic development with considerable humor.

First, the academic world cautiously puts forward qualified theories based on data that is often fragmentary or uncertain. Then, politicians, their advisers, the economic and financial world, and the press appropriate those theories—when they are convenient for them—and transform them into clear assertions. Does that not amount to transforming academic speculation into political action? That implies simple truths expressed with conviction!

Provided that those theories emerge during a period of uncertainty, that they broadly address the concerns of the moment and attract eloquent advocates, the second stage is entered, in which a fashion phenomenon is created. The views expressed by influential figures who see, read, and rub shoulders with one another in the political and economic microcosm become similar if not identical. This strengthens their individual convictions. As Krugman sees it: "People believe certain stories because everyone important tells them and people tell those stories because everyone important believes them." The sphere of rational analysis gradually gives way to that of generally accepted ideas, conventional wisdom, slogans, and myths. Such myths may sometimes mobilize people; and mobilizing myths are essential in politics.

In the final stage, the assertion becomes an article of faith. Anyone departing from the "correct view" is suspected of heresy, or at least a lack of earnest. Says Krugman, "Agreement with conventional wisdom becomes almost a litmus test of one's suitability to be taken seriously."

When the passage of time, irreducible facts, or a major catastrophe demonstrate that the reality is in fact different from the theory, doubt sets in. Accepted truths are rejected. Others are sought, and the cycle begins anew.

Professors of economics may discuss the validity of that theory put forward by Krugman. For my part, I shall confine myself to examining its application to the history of the European integration process.

The consensus of the European political world during the immediate postwar years related primarily to the benefits of opening up markets. That was certainly what motivated the European venture, as its declared object was the creation of a common market, managed, in the interests of efficiency, by an original set of common institutions. The failure of the protectionist policies of the 1930s had left its mark. In particular, it had prompted the Benelux countries, even prior to the end of World War II, to set up amongst themselves an initial structure for economic integration.

The example of the big U.S. market, which dominated the post-war world economy, demonstrated the advantages of productivity, scale, and dynamism that could be gained by opening up the segregated markets of the European countries. In February 1956, Spaak wrote to Anthony Eden, who was then prime minister of the United Kingdom, to try to persuade him to join or at least not oppose the negotiations that culminated in the Treaty of Rome: "To obtain the results of technological progress, of increased production and productivity, and of automation, vast markets are required. The Americans have acquired a standard of living far superior to that of European countries. Russia has announced a new five-year plan." The word *competitiveness* was of course less commonly used than it is today. Nevertheless, the concept that it embraces is very much in evidence.

However, the opening up of markets and the benefits of economic liberalism were just two aspects of the political consensus of the time. The role of the state in the economy, social protection, and cooperation between social partners were also part of it. Alongside economic competitiveness, social cohesion and solidarity were on the agenda. The action of the invisible hand of the market, much beloved of Adam Smith, the eighteenth-century political economist, had to be completed by that of a hand extended in solidarity and at least partially directed or concerted. This was the *soziale Marktwirtschaft*, which governed the spectacular recovery of the German economy.

Monnet recalls in his memoirs how he set up an Allied Military Transport Executive in 1917, which was in fact responsible for managing, in an authoritarian manner and on behalf of the allied forces, supplies for France and for the armies operating there. One cannot help but notice that this international, autonomous, and powerful executive was almost a first sketch of what would later be the Commission. This chapter of his memoirs is entitled "Joint Action," an expression that recurs in the Maastricht Treaty, albeit in a different context. Monnet, who was appointed head of the economic and social development plan in France by de Gaulle in 1946, was openly in favor of a substantial government role in managing the economy. That approach was shared by virtually all leaders of the time, both public and private, and on both sides of the Atlantic.

That was the climate in which the European Community was born. The "founding fathers," most of whom belonged to the Christian Democrat or Socialist Parties of Europe, had in mind a Keynesian economic and social model far removed from conventional liberalism. The dominant role of the state in managing the war economies of both victors and vanquished remained close at hand. The consensus attributed an extensive and vital role in economic development and social regulation to the public authorities, and hence also to the European authority. Europe wanted to consider itself both competitive and bound by solidarity.

F rom the point of view of Krugman's theories, that consensus proved remarkably effective and enduring. For several decades, Europe rebuilt and subsequently developed and diversified its production machine. It increased its productivity and standard of living. It gradually reduced the technological gap between itself and the United States, thus responding to the "American challenge" to which Jean-Jacques Servan-Schreiber referred in his best-selling book.

That the crushed and powerless Europe of 1945 recovered its status as a world player is largely attributable to the opening of markets, which stimulated its economy. After the Marshall Plan, the European Community was the driving force behind that opening process. The creation of the internal market between 1985 and 1992, which was crowned by the single currency in 1999, was simply the fulfillment of an ambition that had already appeared in the very first European texts.

However, alongside that concern for liberalization, and the four freedoms that constitute the single market (goods, services, persons, and capital), the Community has been driven at each stage of its development by a concern for solidarity. There are numerous examples of this: the solidarity between industrialists in the provisions on "manifest crises" in the coal and steel treaty; between rural and urban life in the sustaining of prices under the agricultural policy; between unequally developed areas in the regional policy; between currencies in the "mutual assistance" of the European monetary system. The Single European Act reinforced and transformed the regional policy, turning it into a cohesion policy backed up by substantial means. The Maastricht Treaty created a cohesion fund and introduced a social protocol signed by eleven member states, which the Amsterdam Treaty has incorporated into Community law. It is undoubtedly that solidarity that has enabled the European integration process to gain widespread support over the years, transcending sector-based interests, social classes, and relative levels of development. "The European countries have always attributed a high value to social cohesion and to solidarity," states the first Ciampi report on competitiveness, published in 1995.

The consensus that has made that success possible has inevitably been challenged. It was challenged at the outset by those who feared the immediate effects of the opening up of markets. The Belgian coal mines opposed the coal and steel treaty, and French employers rejected the Treaty of Rome. For many years, much of the industrial sector remained wary of new initiatives inspired by Monnet. That protectionist opposition gradually subsided. It is now nonexistent.

The consensus was challenged more fundamentally by those who feared the institutional machinery, long views, and common policies: in other words, everything that made it possible, beyond a free trade area, to establish a genuine Community that included an element of solidarity.

This challenge often had British origins. During the 1950s, the United Kingdom used all its economic and political weight, which was then considerable, to substitute for the nascent Community a free trade area, namely, "a grouping with vague structures and essentially commercial aims" (Monnet 1976). Because that debate did not prevent the creation of the Community, Britain first established then abandoned the European Free Trade Association, which was to provide a counterweight against the Community vision. After its belated entry into the Community, Britain never really supported the underlying consensus. It presented the Community to British public opinion as a purely economic and commercial entity. It refused to adopt the Social Charter in 1989, and likewise the Protocol on Social Policy in 1992. It has always been critical of the cost and even the principle of the policies of solidarity (agricultural policy, regional policy). It has never ceased, particularly since Margaret Thatcher's speech at Bruges in 1988, to promote the idea of a less closely knit and more extensive Europe, more akin to the free trade area that it always favored.

However, despite the controversies and challenges, the fact remains that over a period of forty years, the European treaties reflect that dual dimension of competitiveness and solidarity that formed the consensus from the start. The Maastricht Treaty established economic and monetary union, which is consistent with the logic of the market and of competitiveness, but it also established the cohesion fund and the social protocol, which belong to the logic of solidarity. The Treaty of Amsterdam consolidates the free movement of persons, particularly by incorporating the Schengen agreements into Community law, but it also inserts the social protocol into the treaty and confers a wider role on the Community with regard to employment policy. The relative weight of the two orientations is debatable, but one cannot deny the coexistence of those two dimensions in the European texts, from the oldest to the most recent.

O ver the past few years, the beginnings of another consensus have emerged and developed, based on a strictly and exclusively liberal vision. The opening of markets, the pursuit of competitiveness, deregulation, and the privatization of public bodies appear to have become targets in themselves, whereas in the traditional vision of the Community they could be part of a balanced whole. In some respects, the reasoning behind that liberal approach is similar to that which underpinned the idea of a free trade area in the 1950s.

The reasons for that change of thinking have been studied extensively and learnedly: the triumph of liberal ideology following the demise of communism, globalization of the economy, dematerialization of economic activity through computer science, and new technologies. In the United States, these new elements were perceived as being fundamentally beneficial, confirming the ideological, economic, technological, and political preeminence of the U.S. model. That has not been the case in Europe. The apparently inexorable rise of unemployment has brought into question the validity of the traditional approach combining competitiveness with solidarity. Relocations and closures of industrial concerns, which are sometimes deeply rooted in the social fabric, cast doubt, in a spectacular manner, on the very foundations of the European model. The prospects for the future are worrying, and for good reason; and they generate that sense of uncertainty that Krugman identifies as being propitious to the birth of a new consensus.

The neoliberal approach may seem dominant today. Indeed, for some people it constitutes an actual dogma—a "correct view" in which competitiveness is no longer perceived as a necessary means but as the key ingredient of a new ideology. In reality, that ideology is strongly contested. It is contested by the labor force, as illustrated at the beginning of 1997 by the spectacular reaction of the trade unions to the closure of the Renault plant in Vilvorde, Belgium. It is also contested by intellectuals of all creeds. Some denounce its simplism: "We cannot all be competitive against each other" (Brittan 1993). Some highlight its subjacent aggressiveness: "It is based essentially on the idea that our economies and societies are already waging a technological, industrial and economic war on all sides" (Lisbon Group 1995). Others point to its lack of perspective: "As a vision of society, it seems too narrow, defective in its social and political assumptions, lacking a sense of history" (Pfaff 1996).

That opposition is not confined to Europe. In 1996, a debate was sparked by an article published in *Foreign Affairs* and written by Ethan Kapstein, the director of New York's prestigious Council on Foreign Relations. He denounced the risks of a policy that creates a large number of losers but only a small number of winners, and he emphasized that "the appropriate goal of economic policy is to improve the lives of the citizenry." Michel Camdessus, the director general of the International Monetary Fund, which is the home seat of international liberalism, observes that "the issue of the actual objectives of economic activity arises everywhere, even where the market economy has triumphed." George Soros, who is familiar with the financial markets, having earned a fortune from them, denounces the insistence on competition as the sole mainspring of social evolution. That "social Darwinism," he says, is based on an erroneous view of reality: "The main point that I wish to emphasise is that co-operation is as much a part of the system as competition."

From the point of view of our reasoning, the important thing is not to establish whether a neoliberal consensus exists, let alone to discuss its merits, but to observe that it is not the approach of the European Community. It is not the approach of the treaties. In 1993, it was not the approach of the Commission's white paper on growth, competitiveness, and employment. "It offers a concrete utopia for the Europe of the future" (Sweeney 1996). In 1995 and 1996, it was not the approach of the consultative group on competitiveness (the Ciampi group), which stated in its report that "Europe must find its way within the framework of a social model based on consensus, compromise and participation." The opinion given by the Commission on the eve of the intergovernmental conference in 1996 was more precise: "The European venture combines the features of democracy with those of an open economy based on a dynamic market, solidarity and cohesion." That statement contains the two orientations that have characterized the Community's traditional approach since the beginning.

However, the public's perception of European affairs is determined by the vital importance that is rightly attributed to economic and monetary union. In several member states, it has been, for some years, the government's main political objective. That has focused public attention on the Maastricht criteria. They were initially a measuring instrument and have since become a fetish. The budgetary discipline that stems from them appears to have moved ahead of all other concerns. Public opinion has reached the conclusion that the European integration process is now to be inspired solely by the law of the market and by its constraints. The Council's refusal to take appropriate action on the basis of the Commission white paper produced by Delors in 1993 has reinforced that impression. The concern for competitiveness and the will to reduce public expenditure appear to exclude the implementation of joint action. That is not what the treaties say. Neither is it what the Community does in many spheres. But "in politics, it is not raw facts that count, but the perception one has of them" (Duhamel 1995).

The issue, however, is not primarily one of perception but of substance. Community life is not dominated, as some people seem to believe, by an ultraliberal philosophy in which solidarity is a minor concern. Its approach is far more balanced, but that balance is fragile. It embraces a fundamental problem, which is a problem of society. How can the European social model, which was a product of the postwar period, be adapted to the new aspects of the world economy?

Two considerations dominate that debate. First, the globalization of the economy, the free movement of capital, the rise of highly competitive Asian economies, the computerization of society, technological development, and the aging of the population create a strategic problem for European society. Second, in that open and globalized context, which is very different than the postwar context, it is the dynamics of the spirit of enterprise and competition, and thus the private sector, that holds most of the control levers in connection with financial movements, industrial locations, research, and hence innovation.

Therefore, competition is guaranteed; but how can solidarity be provided?

Simply to maintain the traditional social model, which marked the birth and growth of the Community, is not an adequate solution. The immediate results show that it leads to a level of unemployment that is higher in Western Europe than elsewhere.

To dismantle that social model completely, which would be the answer of the neoliberal orthodoxy, is politically unacceptable in virtually all member states. It would bring into question the very essence of European society.

What compromise would allow most of the European social contract to be maintained, while facing up to the internal and external challenges? Many studies have been elaborated, and many scenarios sketched out. No model has gained universal support or even produced the beginnings of a consensus. "Indeed what is lacking in Europe is a viable political strategy for renegotiating the postwar bargain" (Kapstein 1996).

Without playing at strategists, we can perhaps make two observations.

First, a globalized economy implies actors on a world level who are able to argue their point of view in a planetary dialogue. In the private sector, those actors exist in the form of large multinational corporations. They are beginning to appear in the public sector, too, in the form of regional entities, such as the European Union, that are able to exercise a joint regulatory power.

It is not only in Europe that regional groupings are trying to establish themselves. Admittedly, as pointed out by the Lisbon Group, "No single example of a regional economic unit is truly comparable to others." However, there are signs that this regional approach may develop to such an extent that it becomes the dominant form of organization in the world economy. That is a weighty argument in favor of European integration.

Second, if the European countries wish to reform their social model, which seems inevitable, they will only be able to do so effectively by acting together, given the interdependency of their economies. That is a further argument in favor of European integration.

This implies a slight but genuine increase in the role of the Community in coordinating both economic and employment policies. That is one of the new dimensions introduced by the Treaty of Amsterdam. It also implies a joint approach, confined if need be to certain member states, to defining a social and economic model that is appropriate to European society, which may not be the model that is appropriate elsewhere. This issue of a joint approach was raised during the negotiation of the Maastricht Treaty, as a counterpart of the competence granted to the European Central Bank in the monetary domain. The question was not resolved before Maastricht or indeed before Amsterdam. It will not be resolved until a political consensus or at least a strong majority view is established as to the social model and hence, in effect, as to the purpose of the Union. That opinion is gradually taking shape. We must help it to grow.

Chapter 10

THE END
AND THE MEANS

 For more than thirty years, the participating countries have abstained from raising among themselves the fundamental questions of the purposes of European integration. What is the ultimate goal of the exercise? What model are we heading toward? How far do our ambitions extend?

The negotiation of the Fouchet plan in 1961 and 1962 brought de Gaulle's vision of a Europe of homelands (*Europe des patries*) face to face with the supranational vision defended in different ways by France's partners. This was a turning point in the European integration process—one of the rare occasions on which the topic of ultimate aims has been clearly raised. De Gaulle wanted to set up "organised and regular consultation between the responsible governments." Jean Monnet's "Action Committee," which was exercising a considerable influence on European politics at the time, wanted to save the existing communities and to keep open the option of evolving toward a federal system.

On both sides, the convictions were strong, as were the interests at stake; there was extreme wariness and little inclination to compromise. Under those circumstances, failure was almost inevitable, and perhaps even desired. Spaak suspected Couve de Murville, who presided over the final stage of the negotiation conference, of having deliberately led it to a dead end. But the causes are of lesser importance. The fact is that coming a few years after the failure of the European Defense Community and that of the European Political Community, the failure of the Fouchet plan had lasting psychological and political consequences. The conclusion drawn was that any discussion of aims and purposes led the partners into insoluble and futile debates. It would bring profound differences to the surface, without benefiting anyone and without making Europe progress.

By contrast, accepting a degree of ambiguity, a pragmatic approach focusing on deadlines, procedures, and specific objectives for the short or medium term allowed progress without making waves.

That had already been Spaak's attitude in negotiating the Treaty of Rome: "Our ambitions were modest. So too were our hopes." That was the approach of the first documents on political cooperation, and of the Tindemans report in 1975: "Any other approach, because of its utopian nature in the present circumstances, would lose all credibility with the parties in power." The same applies to the Stuttgart declaration in 1983, the Single European Act in 1986, and the Maastricht Treaty in 1992. In the latter case, the preamble of the draft treaty submitted to the European Council in December 1991 suggested that the Union should be assigned a "federal vocation," which could be considered as a first sketch of what the future might hold. Those words were removed by the heads of government at Maastricht itself, under pressure from Britain and with little debate; such was the strength of the conviction that all discussion on the ultimate goals of the Union is futile. The negotiators of the Treaty of Amsterdam did not even try to express an ambition of that kind in a preamble.

"Having no shared vision, nor even any clear and consensual individual perspective of the future of the European venture, the States have preferred to regard it as a pragmatic process with an undetermined and perpetually deferred end-point" (Cohen-Tanugi 1995).

There is no doubt that this approach involving small steps, no long-term visions, and no great leaps has had considerable merits. It has enabled Europe to move forward. Today's Europe is very different from the Europe of the 1960s. Progress has been possible in spite of ongoing disagreement between the supporters of integration and the supporters of cooperation, between partisans of a "Community" and those who prefer a "common market," or even an "area." It has enabled successive enlargements to be negotiated without too much quarreling. It has allowed time, which has changed mentalities to such an extent that in the eyes of a new generation, Europe seems self-evident. It has rendered the integration process if not irreversible, then at least difficult to turn back.

However, that approach obviously has a political cost.

"We are in a binding and illegible system in which nobody can distinguish the end from the means anymore" (Thibaud 1995). By obscuring objectives so as to focus on instruments, Europe has denied itself a justification and hence an element of legitimacy. To adapt the means to the ends that one is pursuing is the very essence of the art of politics. And, in a democracy, those ends must be known and publicly accepted. How can they be accepted if they are not discussed?

Under those circumstances, public opinion is divided between incomprehension and indifference. The Europe of visionaries, general ideas, grand designs, and great ambitions certainly exists in the minds of some people, but it is left to one side, passed over without comment, or put away in the utopia box. All that we see today is the Europe of regulations, directives, and complex procedures—in other words, the Europe of technocrats and administrators. We see the *how* but not the *why*. No explicit political justification, no mobilizing myth, no symbols, and thus no emotion, little enthusiasm, and scarcely any passion.

That may suffice if one wishes to consider European integration as having no other aim than the management of interdependencies. But as with any policy, it is also a matter of people: "The reality of politics and policies is more than a complex system of functionalist management of socio-economic interdependencies and power relations. It is also a field of communication and interaction between human beings, groups, communities, regions and nations, on what is important, what is meaningful and what should be done and pursued." How can one not subscribe to that view expressed by Professor Heinrich Schneider of the University of Vienna?

Technocratic Europe, the Europe of procedures and regulations, can be accepted or rejected; but one cannot deny that it is present in the political life of member states. Neither can one deny that it often proves to be efficient, which has many advantages. The Europe of people, of citizens, is largely absent from the political debate, which has many disadvantages. There comes a time when the disadvantages outweigh the advantages. When does that time come? That is a matter of political judgment. Some would say it has already been reached. Others would prefer to carry on as before.

European integration has focused on markets: first the common market, then the internal market. It has attached considerable importance to setting up policies—agriculture, industry, trade, regional development. It also extends to research, the environment, fishing, and finally currency. It has developed intergovernmental cooperation on foreign policy and internal security, and has endeavored to incorporate or at least connect that cooperation into the Community's institutional machinery. All that is fundamental for the future; but the markets, the policies, and the various forms of cooperation will only ever be instruments, even in the case of foreign policy or currency. What aims are they to serve? The absence of a reply to that question and the confusion that is maintained between the end and the means, the objectives and the instruments, constitute a great weakness. They make Europe "a soulless body with an obscure destiny" (Duverger 1994).

Without a vision of the future there can be no strategy. This applies to political constructions just as it does to industrial or commercial enterprises. Philippe de Woot, an expert on business management, wrote that "a shared tangible vision creates a situation where the enterprise is being pulled by the future instead of being pushed by the past." To turn to the future rather than to the past has, after all, been the Community's approach from the outset. Is the Community still fueled by a shared tangible vision? How can that vision be defined?

The actual history of the Community can of course serve as a guide. The trodden path reveals a direction. A structure of such complexity is not created by chance. It reflects a shared intention: the will to face up to the challenges of the moment and to the lessons of history. It implies an ambition, and therefore a goal, even though the meaning and scope of the venture have, to some extent, been dimmed by the passage of time and the lack of debate. "Europe now needs to recover a line of thought" (Giscard d'Estaing 1995).

The preceding pages were intended to direct the reader's mind along paths on which certain elements of that line of thought can be found. The apparatus is action orientated by means of an original and efficient institutional and legal structure. The idea is to manage certain resources and policies together while respecting the identity of nations and without excessive intervention, and maintaining the cohesion and solidarity of the Union, its openness to the rest of the world, its competitiveness, and hence its prosperity. It is to exercise a collective power in world affairs, jointly and peacefully. Peace, prosperity, and power!

Taking the reasoning a step further, one might say that the aim of the joint venture pursued in Western Europe for almost half a century has been to develop a model of society. "The sense of a shared destiny, based on one same vision of mankind, represents both the cause and the condition of common policy and common legislation" (Millon-Delsol 1993).

Models of society are distinguished from one another primarily through the different relations that they establish between the individual and the collective, or between individual interests and the general interest. From that point of view, the European model is entirely different from its Asian, Islamic, or African counterparts. As a result of its historic consanguinity, it is close to the U.S. model, but it differs from that model through its emphasis on solidarity and social protection, and through the diversity of its constituent parts.

Diversity is clearly one of the keys to European society. It is already very prominent, and sometimes a source of conflict inside many of the member states. Within the Union it is structural, and it gives the Union its singular nature. The bonds created by history and the upholding of shared values coexist with cultural diversity and national identities. That is reflected in multiple attachments, a plurality of allegiances, and diverse sources of legitimacy.

To ensure that this coexistence would be peaceful and respectful, which it had not always been in the past, was one of the primary goals of the European integration process. To defend diversity against the standardizing pressures of globalization, computerization, and technology is undoubtedly another, more recent goal. Like other states before them, the European states are discovering that their diversity can only be defended through a joint effort.

Pursuing that reasoning to its conclusion, one could say that the gradual development of the European structure does in fact reveal an ultimate goal, even though that goal remains largely unformulated. It is to establish a political and legal structure responsible for maintaining, developing, and defending a model of society that is specific to the participating countries. They base that model on a number of political considerations, such as diversity, and on certain ethical values, such as solidarity, which they essentially share. "Societies gain their cohesion from shared values. Those values are rooted in culture, religion, history and tradition" (Soros 1997).

Although those aims are implicit in the historic development of the Community, they are not expressly stated anywhere. The validity of the reasoning through which they are identified is far from being universally accepted. Even some of those who recognize its validity differ as to the conclusions to be drawn from it, the implementation of these conclusions, and the institutional machinery required for that purpose. All discussion on that subject turns to discord. To conceal those differences and to prevent discord, the debate is avoided. And without a debate, one loses the support of public opinion, which is needed if the objectives are to be attained. How can one escape that contradiction?

The most obvious solution lies in organizing difference. Because the member states have conflicting views on the future of Europe, let us organize different Europes to address them! That, after all, is what the founders did when they broke away from the Council of Europe.

The idea of structuring the Union as a group of differentiated zones is not new, for it underpins the provisions of the Maastricht Treaty concerning economic and monetary union. The European structure has always been more flexible than it is said to be. But to make that approach systematic, no longer a last resort but normal practice, by taking steps yet to be defined (and that vary considerably from one opinion to the next), is neither simple nor without danger for the cohesion of the Union. All discussions on this matter are full of unspoken reservations. Nevertheless, it is no doubt the only way to reconcile, across the entire continent, the diversity of the states' respective situations and ambitions with coherent pursuit of the European idea. "In fact, the choice is not between different forms of differentiation, but between differentiation and scattering" (Club de Florence 1996). That new and hence suspicious subject played an important role in the negotiations leading up to the Treaty of Amsterdam, though it had been excluded by the reflection group that was set up prior to the negotiations. Time will tell whether the solutions adopted in that treaty will satisfy expectations.

A differentiated approach to European integration, allowing reinforced cooperation between certain member states, is particularly beneficial in that it provides a better approach to the difficult problems associated with an increase in the number of participants. Between 1993 and 1995, Europe took a major political turning—certainly as important as that of Maastricht—without any real internal debate and without challenge. The positions adopted within the European Council in a series of meetings beginning with the Copenhagen meeting of June 1993, have made it inevitable that the European Union will eventually enlarge as far as the old frontiers of the Soviet Union, and even a little beyond, in that the Baltic states are to be included. That decision was perceived by the heads of government as a moral duty and a political imperative. It is obviously irreversible. Can one imagine that the leaders of the Central and Eastern European states, having been invited to attend the meetings of the European Council on a regular basis for several years, and having been photographed together with its members in the most prestigious locations, might one day be told that they do not belong to the club and must abandon the idea of joining it? That is morally and politically unthinkable.

The attitude of the European Council reflects the fact that for Europe the problem of enlargement is a problem unlike all others. In a way, it concerns the actual aims of the enterprise, and, on that subject, it has long been agreed that there should be no discussion. Would the European integration process not lose some of its meaning if countries that are plainly European and display a clear and sometimes embarrassing will to join were deliberately excluded from the process?

The increased diversity of an enlarged European Union accentuates the need for differentiated solutions. The experience of German reunification has demonstrated that despite the unity of both language and nation, and despite the investment of huge sums, it takes more than a few months to erase forty years of separate history. The Union must learn to adapt its structure to suit its own diversity. The issue is not exclusively linked to enlargement, because the problem arises already. "Increased use of differentiation is not only a necessity in view of further enlargements. The problem of deepening already exists within the Union of fifteen member States" (Ehlermann 1995).

A diversified Europe will no doubt be more complex. Will it be more obscure, more distant, and even less legible? That need not be the case. Provided that we seize the opportunity to enter into a real debate, to discuss our different views, to define political objectives, and group together those who share them, it should be possible to give a meaning and thus a soul to an enterprise that currently seems to have none. Enlargement carries a risk of dilution. Conversely, it may also provide the opportunity to gather together, from both East and West, those who share a political ambition and accept its constraints.

O ver the years, Europe has built a skeleton: its strong, original, and durable institutional structure. It has acquired common policies that can be likened to the flesh that clads the skeleton and the blood that irrigates the various parts of the body. Admittedly, a number of useless bulges appear here and there, and an obvious lack of muscle sometimes makes for unsteady progress. However, the existence of that body is clear, unchallenged, and recognized by third parties. Does that body possess a soul, or a spirit? The question is seldom raised, and the answer is therefore less clear.

To most people, the European structure embodies economic aims and material values: industry, agriculture, fishing, finance, energy, communications, research. Yet from the very start, it has also conveyed immaterial values: peace and security, solidarity and cohesion, integration without hegemony, respect for diversity, subsidiarity. By turning the economic Community into a European Union, the Maastricht Treaty merely evokes the initial ambition and confirms a long-standing orientation. But that orientation and that ambition usually go unnoticed. In the eyes of public opinion, these immaterial values seem either self-evident or unimportant. But are they not the essence?

"Vivitur ingenio caetera mortis erunt": one lives through the spirit, the rest belongs to death. That was the motto of Willibald Pirckheimer, patrician of Nuremberg, humanist and warrior, who lived from 1470 to 1530 and who would now be entirely forgotten had he not decided to have his portrait engraved by Albrecht Dürer, who was his closest friend. Is it not time to engrave the traits of our future Europe somewhere? And to show that it possesses a soul, or a spirit, so that it may live!

B ILIBALDI · PIRKEYMHERI · EFFIGIES
· AETATIS · SVAE · ANNO · L · iii ·
VIVITVR · INGENIO · CAETERA · MORTIS ·
ERVNT ·
· M · D · X X · i V ·

BIBLIOGRAPHY

Chapter 1: Concept and Action

Burke, Edmund. 1790. *Reflections on the Revolution in France*. London, p. 88.

Churchill, Winston. 1948. Letter of 25 April to Stafford Cripps. Cited by Peter Hennessy in *Never Again*. London: Jonathan Cape, 1992, p. 359.

de Gaulle, Charles. 1950. Speech given in Metz, 17 May. Cited by Jean Monnet in *Mémoires*. Paris: Fayard, 1976, pp. 634–635.

———. 1960. Speech broadcast on radio and television, 31 May. Cited by Jean-Claude Masclet in *L'Union politique de l'Europe*. Paris: P.U.F., 1990, p. 38.

Le Goff, Jacques. 1994. *La vieille Europe et la nôtre*. Paris: Seuil, p. 7.

Millon-Delsol, Chantal. 1993. *Le principe de subsidiarité*. Paris: P.U.F., p. 93.

Monnet, Jean. 1976. *Mémoires*. Paris: Fayard, pp. 412, 441.

Spaak, Paul Henri. 1969. *Combats inachevés*. Paris: Fayard, tome II, pp. 50, 52, 100.

———. Article published in *Le Soir*, 8 June 1950. Reproduced in *La pensée européenne et atlantique de Paul-Henri Spaak*. Bruxelles: Goemaere, 1980, tome I, p. 223.

Chapter 2: Empire and Nation

De Gaulle, Charles. 1970. "Mémoires d'Espoir." Paris. Plon. Vol. 1, p. 206.

Dehaene, Jean-Luc. 1995. Speech given 13 January at the College of Europe in Natolin.

Delors, Jacques. 1992. Speech given 7 September at the London Forum on Europe and the World. *Agence Europe.* Europe Documents, No. 1795, 10 September.

Duhamel, Alain. 1995. *La politique imaginaire.* Paris: Flammarion, p. 257.

Duverger, Maurice. 1994. *Europe des hommes.* Paris: Odile Jacob, p. 61.

Fukuyama, Francis. 1989. "La fin de l'histoire?" *Commentaire* 12, no. 47 (Automne).

Ganshof, François. 1953. *Le moyen âge.* Tome I of *L'Histoire des relations internationales,* Pierre Renouvin, ed. Paris: Hachette, p. 306.

de Gaulle, Charles. 1970. *Mémoires d'espoir.* Paris: Plon, tome I, p. 206.

Kohl, Helmut. 1996. Speech given 2 February at the University of Louvain.

Le Goff, Jacques. 1994. *La vieille Europe et la nôtre.* Paris: Seuil, p. 62.

Malraux, André. 1976. *Le miroir des limbes.* Paris: Editions de la Pléiade, p. 699.

Mitterand, François. 1995. Speech given 17 January to the European Parliament in Strasbourg.

Monnet, Jean. 1976. *Mémoires.* Paris: Fayard, p. 407.

Sellier, Jean and André. 1995. *Atlas des peuples d'Europe occidentale.* Paris: La Découverte, p. 9.

Spaak, Paul Henri. 1969. *Combats inachevés.* Paris: Fayard, tome II, p. 99.

Thibaud, Paul. 1995. *Et maintenant.* Paris: Arlea, p. 124.

Tugendhat, Christopher. 1986. *Making Sense of Europe.* London: Viking Penguin, p. 6.

Chapter 3: Structure and Network

Duhamel, Alain. 1995. *La politique imaginaire.* Paris: Flammarion, p. 9.

Fontaine, Pascal. 1990. "Une idée neuve pour l'Europe: La déclaration Schuman," *Documentation Européenne,* no. 3 (1990).

Guéhenno, Jean-Marie. 1993. *La fin de la démocratie.* Paris: Flammarion, pp. 74, 82.

Hoffmann, Stanley. 1999. In *The Dynamics of Western European Integration,* edited by William Wallace. London: Pinter, p. 282.

Moreau-Desfarges, Philippe. 1985. In *La relance de l'UEO, implications pour la CE et ses institutions,* edited by Tsakaloyanis. Maastricht: European Institute for Public Administration, pp. 49, 50.

Sbragia, Alberta.1992. *Europolitics.* Washington, D.C.: The Brookings Institution, p. 262.

Thibaud, Paul. 1995. *Et maintenant.* Paris: Alea, p. 57.

Wallace, William. 1990. *The Transformation of Western Europe.* London: Pinter, p. 95.

Chapter 4: Law and Politics

Duverger, Maurice. 1994. *Europe des hommes.* Paris: Odile Jacob, pp. 131–132.
de Gaulle, Charles. 1970. *Mémoires d'espoir.* Paris: Plon, tome I, p. 188.
Isaac, Guy. 1994. *Droit communautaire général.* 4th ed. Paris: Masson, p. 167.
Judgment of the Court of Justice. 1964. *Costa* v. *ENEL.* Case 6/64, 15 July.
Pescatore, Pierre. 1975. *L'ordre juridique des Communautés européennes.* Liège: Presses Universitaires, p. 257.
Spaak, Paul Henri. 1969. *Combats inachevés.* Paris: Fayard, tome II, p. 72.
Thibaud, Paul. 1995. *Et maintenant.* Paris: Arlea, p. 43.

Chapter 5: Subsidiarity and Intervention

Cot, Jean-Pierre. 1990. Quoted by *Le Monde,* 22 June.
Delors, Jacques. 1992. *Le nouveau concert européen.* Paris: Odile Jacob, pp. 147, 176, 316.
Millon-Delsol, Chantal. 1993. *Le principe de subsidiarité.* Paris: P.U.F., p. 95.
Tocqueville, Alexis de. 1991–1992. *Rapport sur la démocratie en Suisse* and *De la démocratie en Amérique.* Editions de la Pléiade. Paris: Gallimard, tome I, p. 640, tome II, p. 126.

Chapter 6: Democracy and Communication

Club de Florence. 1996. *Europe: L'Impossible statu quo.* Paris: Stock, p. 257.
European Round Table of Industrialists. 1995. "Education for Europeans. Towards the Learning Society" (February), p. 18.
Fukuyama, Francis. 1995. "Social Capital and the Global Economy." *Foreign Affairs* 74 (September–October), p. 103.

Guéhenno, Jean-Marie. 1993. *La fin de la démocratie*. Paris: Flammarion, p. 47.

Sellier, Jean and André. 1996. *Atlas de l'Europe occidentale*. Paris: Librairie Européenne des Idées, p. 7.

Sung, Tzu-wen. 1972. "L'Art de la guerre." Paris: Flammarion, p. 96.

Wolton, Dominique. 1993. *La dernière utopie*. Paris: Flammarion, pp. 175, 177, 194.

Chapter 7: Cohesion and Diversity

Benelux Memorandum. 1996. Agence Europe. No. 6684, 9 March.

Chirac, Jacques, and Helmut Kohl. 1995. Letter to European Council. *Agence Europe,* Europe Documents, No. 6622, 9 December.

Club de Florence. 1996. *Europe: L'impossible statu quo*. Paris: Stock, pp. 224, 237–238.

Delors Jacques. 1991. Speech given 12 December to the European Parliament. Reproduced in *Le nouveau concert européen*. Paris: Odile Jacob, 1992, p. 178.

Millon-Delsol, Chantal. 1993. *Le principe de subsidiarité*. Paris: P.U.F., p. 94.

Peyrefitte, Alain. 1992. Welcoming speech given 12 December for Jean Deniau at the Académie Française.

Tindemans, Léo. 1975. "Report on the European Union." *Bulletin of the European Communities*. Supplement 1/76.

Chapter 8: Power and Impotence

Cohen-Tanugi, Laurent. 1995. *Le Choix de l'Europe*. Paris: Fayard, p. 84.

Delors, Jacques. 1991. Speech given 7 March at the Institute for Strategic Studies in London. Reproduced in *Le nouveau concert européen*. Paris: Odile Jacob, p. 301.

———. 1994. *L'Unité d'un homme*. Paris: Odile Jacob, p. 241.

Duhamel, Alain. 1995. *La politique imaginaire*. Paris: Flammarion, p. 264.

Eizenstat, Stuart. 1996. *Financial Times*. 16 February.

European Round Table of Industrialists. 1991. "Reshaping Europe" (September), p. 46.

Froment-Meurice, Henri. 1984. *Une puissance nommée Europe*. Paris: Julliard, p. 157.

Gnesotto, Nicole. 1996. *Libération.* 8 October.

Holbrooke, Richard. 1995. "America, A European Power." *Foreign Affairs* 74, no. 2 (March–April), p. 38.

Mitterrand, François. 1995. Speech given 17 January to the European Parliament in Strasbourg.

Monnet, Jean. 1976. *Mémoires.* Paris: Fayard. pp. 417–418.

Rummel, Reinhardt. 1997. In *Foreign Policy of the European Union.* London: Lynne Rienner, pp. 371, 377.

Schuman, Robert. 1976. Cited by Jean Monnet in *Mémoires.* Paris: Fayard, 1976, p. 441.

Spaak, Paul Henri. 1969. *Combats inachevés.* Paris: Fayard, tome II, p. 52.

Tindemans, Léo. Report on the European Communities. *Bulletin of the European Communities.* Supplement 1/76.

Wörner, Manfred. 1991. (Speech reproduced in *Agence Europe.*) Colloque du Parti Populaire Européen. *Agence Europe,* 3 July.

Chapter 9: Competition and Solidarity

Brittan, Samuel. 1993. "The Myth of European Competitiveness." *Financial Times,* 1 July.

Camdessus, Michel. 1996. *Le Monde,* 18 January.

Duhamel, Alain. 1995. *La politique imaginaire.* Paris: Flammarion, p. 7.

"Improving European Competitiveness." 1995. Consultative Group's first and third report on competitiveness to the president of the Commission and to the heads of state and government (June), p. 4.

Kapstein, Ethan. 1996. "Workers and the World Economy." *Foreign Affairs* 75, no. 3 (May–June), p. 31. See also the reactions to that article, particularly that of Paul Krugman, in the following edition, and also Kapstein's response, *Foreign Affairs* 75, no. 4 (July–August 1996), pp. 164–181.

Krugman, Paul. 1966. "Cycles of Conventional Wisdom on Economic Development." *International Affairs* 75, no. 1, p. 722. See also by the same author: "The Myth of Asia's Miracle." *Foreign Affairs* 73, no. 6 (November–December 1994).

Lisbon Group. 1995: *Limits to Competition.* Cambridge, Mass.: The M.I.T. Press, p. 115.

Monnet, Jean. 1976. *Mémoires.* Paris: Fayard, p. 667.

"Opinion of the Commission on the Intergovernmental Conference." 1996. *Bulletin of the European Union.* No. 1/2, p. 168.

Pfaff, William. 1996. "Seeking a Broader Vision of Economic Society." *International Herald Tribune,* 3 February.

Soros, George. 1997. "The Capitalist Threat." *Atlantic Monthly* 279, no. 2 (February).

Spaak, Paul Henri. 1969. *Combats inachevés*. Paris: Fayard, tome II, p. 78.

Sweeney, John. 1996. In *Travail et solidarité,* edited by Ignace Berten. Rennes: Edition Apogée, p. 135.

Chapter 10: The End and the Means

Club de Florence. 1996. *Europe: L'Impossible statu quo.* Paris: Stock, p. 238.

Cohen-Tanugi, Laurent. 1995. *Le choix de l'Europe.* Paris: Fayard, p. 168.

Duverger, Maurice. 1994. *L'Europe des hommes.* Paris: Odile Jacob, p. 8.

Ehlermann, Claus Dieter. 1995. "Différenciation accrue ou uniformité renforcée?" *Revue du marché unique européen,* no. 3.

Giscard d'Estaing, Valéry. 1995. "Europe: Les raisons de l'échec." *Le Figaro,* 10 January.

Millon-Delsol, Chantal. 1993. *Le principe de subsidiarité.* Paris: P.U.F., p. 94.

Schneider, Heinrich. 1993. "The Dimension of the Historical and Cultural Core of a European Identity." Bonn: Europäische Schriften des Instituts für Europäische Politik. Vol. 70, p. 282.

Soros, George. 1997. "The Capitalist Threat." *Atlantic Monthly* 279, no. 2 (February).

Spaak, Paul Henri. 1969. *Combats Inachevés.* Paris: Fayard, tome II, p. 62.

Thibaud, Paul. 1995. *Et Maintenant.* Paris: Arlea, p. 35.

Tindemans, Léo. 1975. Introductory letter attached to the report on the European Union. *Bulletin of the European Communities.* Supplement 1/76, 29 December.

de Woot, Philippe. 1996. In *Transforming Organizations,* edited by A. Sinatra. London: Kluwer Academic Publishers.

INDEX

Adenauer, Konrad, 40, 72
Althusius, Johannes, 42
Aristotle, 42

Balladur, Edouard, 68
Bosman, Jean-Marc, 36
Braudel, Fernand, 32
Briand, Aristide, 4
Brittan, Samuel, 91
Burke, Edmund, 9

Camdessus, Michel, 91
Chirac, Jacques, 68
Churchill, Sir Winston, 6, 71
Ciampi, Carlo, 89, 92
Clinton, William ("Bill"), 54
"Club de Florence," 58, 65, 69, 103
Cohen-Tanugi, 76, 99
Cot, Jean-Pierre, 45
Coudenhove-Calergi, Richard, 4
Couve de Murville, Maurice, 37, 98
Cripps, Sir Stafford, 6

Davignon, Etienne, 62, 67, 73
de Gaulle, Charles, 4, 7, 15, 19, 40, 62, 72, 87, 97
Dehaene, Jean-Luc, 20
Delors, Jacques, 16, 43, 44, 46, 55, 60, 65, 74, 76, 77, 92
Duhamel, Alain, 2, 14, 24, 76, 93
Dürer, Albrecht, 106
Duverger, Maurice, 18, 39, 101

Eden, Anthony, 87
Ehlermann, Claus Dieter, 105
Eizenstat, Stuart, 79

Fontaine, Pascal, 25
Fouchet, Christian, 97, 98
Froment-Meurice, Henri, 80
Fukuyama, Francis, 20, 55

Ganshof, François, 15
Genscher, Hans Dietrich, 75
Giscard d'Estaing, Valéry, 18, 44, 64, 68, 101
Gnesotto, Nicole, 80

Gracian, Baltasar, 85
Guéhenno, Jean-Marie, 32, 60

Hallstein, Walter, 17
Hoffmann, Stanley, 31
Holbrooke, Richard, 82

Isaac, Guy, 36

John-Paul II, 42

Kapstein, Ethan, 91, 94
Kohl, Helmut, 20, 68, 78
Kohnstamm, Max, 58
Krugman, Paul, 85, 86, 88, 91

Le Goff, Jacques, 5, 18
Léon XIII, 42
Lincoln, Abraham, 41, 46
"Lisbon Group," the, 91, 94
Livy, 75

Machiavelli, Niccolò, 56
Major, John, 68
Malraux, André, 19
Marshall, George Catlett, 88
Millon-Delsol, Chantal, 3, 43, 61, 102
Mitterand, François, 20, 72, 78
Monnet, Jean, 4, 5, 6, 16, 19, 20, 27, 58, 61, 71, 72, 87, 89, 97
Montaigne, Michel de, 2
Moreau-Desfarges, Philippe, 31, 32

Pericles, 51
Pescatore, Pierre, 35

Peyrefitte, Alain, 62
Pfaff, William, 91
Pirckheimer, Willibald, 106

Retz, Cardinal de, 3
"Round Table of Industrialists," 55, 76
Rousseau, Jean-Jacques, 23
Rummel, Reinhardt, 79

Saint Thomas, 42
Sbragia, Alberta, 32
Schmidt, Helmut, 64
Schneider, Heinrich, 100
Schuman, Robert, 4, 5, 6, 7, 16, 17, 61, 72
Sellier, Jean and André, 55
Seneca, 97
Servan-Schreiber, Jean-Jacques, 88
Smith, Adam, 87
Soros, George, 92, 102
Spaak, Paul Henri, 5, 6, 7, 14, 33, 37, 72, 87, 98
Spinelli, Altiero, 44, 46
Stresemann, Gustave, 4
Sung Tzu-wen, 56
Sweeney, John, 92

Thatcher, Margaret, 46, 90
Thibaud, Paul, 19, 32, 35, 99
Tindemans, Léo, 28, 44, 64, 73, 74, 76, 83, 98
Tocqueville, Charles Alexis de, 43, 56
Toynbee, Arnold, 13, 19
Tugendhat, Christopher, 16

Uri, Pierre, 33

Vauvenargues, Luc de, 33

Waigel, Theo, 65
Wales, HRH The Prince of, 47, 48

Wallace, William, 31
Werner, Pierre, 67
Wolton, Dominique, 55, 57, 58
Woot, Philippe de, 101
Wörner, Manfred, 83

ABOUT THE BOOK

The Case for Europe sets out the basic rationales and characteristics of the process of European integration that we have been witnessing for half a century. Philippe de Schoutheete, for ten years Belgium's permanent representative to the European Union, demystifies the structures of the EU, the basic forces and reasons that make it work, and the strengths and weaknesses of what has been achieved. He also points to the difficult questions the Union now faces: When to act? How best (and whether) to project power? How to respect diversity and reconcile competition and solidarity?

De Schoutheete does not offer simple answers to these questions. But his penetrating analysis looks beyond the facade of institutions and the mountains of paper they produce to illuminate fundamental issues. It has been translated into seven European languages

Ambassador Philippe de Schoutheete de Tervarent served in Belgium's Ministry of Foreign Affairs from 1956 to 1997. He is author of *La coopération politique européenne.* In 1997, he was awarded the Adolphe Bentinck Prize and the Medal of the European Parliament for his contribution to European integration. He is guest professor at the Catholic University of Louvain.